What Makes for the
Joyful and Fulfilling Life?

OF LIFE'S JOURNEY

KAYAN SMITH

WESTBOW
PRESS
A DIVISION OF THOMAS NELSON

ISBN: 978-1-4497-5360-3 (sc)
ISBN: 978-1-4497-5361-0 (e)

Library of Congress Control Number: 2012909177

WestBow Press books may be ordered through booksellers or by contacting:

WestBow Press
A Division of Thomas Nelson
1663 Liberty Drive
Bloomington, IN 47403
www.westbowpress.com
1-(866) 928-1240

Printed in the United States of America

WestBow Press rev. date: 06/05/12

To:

God – my true source of inspiration

Austin and Juliet Smith

All those who have impacted my life, in big and small ways

*Everyone who has played a part in the production
and distribution of this book*

You - my valued reader

Contents

Preface

WHAT MOST OF US have in common is that we're all seeking:

- ways to enhance and preserve our lives
- opportunities to experience the best of life

We all seek joy and fulfillment in life.

There are so many alternatives that provide some sort of solution to this quest. But life itself proves the ineffectiveness of these alternatives.

Many persons have grown frustrated from not being able to perceive any meaning out of their life, regardless of how hard they try to create meanings. There are those who thought, "If only I get that dream job, dream car, dream house, a bigger income, get married and/or have a baby, I'll find real meaning out of life" – Then they got them. Only to find out that these joyful things and events were not sufficient to make them into that genuinely joyful person empowered to live the overall joyful and fulfilling life.

There are many sincere Christians, and sincere people of other religions too, who live pious lives, but are not experiencing the joy and fulfillment that they expected to follow from such a life. There are still those who merely struggle to remain pious because practically, they just have not found much to be desired from their religious experience. In theory their religion seems to work, but not practically for their lives. Or maybe it works for some situations but not all the time; or for some people but not for everyone.

But could it be that something is deficient; something that is the constant solution for all people, throughout all ages; something that is the solution for even your own life? This deficient ingredient, this universal solution, is the Essence of Life's Journey.

What is the Essence of Life's Journey and where can it be found? All of us who have journeyed on this earth have set out, in one way or another, in pursuit of this Essence of Life.

We all crave it, even when we do not know what it is. As a result of this craving, we may set out seeking for it even unconsciously. Many do not have a clue about the nature of it, where to find it or how it can be obtained. However, life tells them that there is more to be obtained in order to bountifully nourish their life's Journey. Whatever that more is, they have this strong instinct that it must be out there - it must be somewhere out there. And it is!

The Essence of Life's Journey nourishes us and illuminates our path for us to live life abundantly. This book explores the Essence of Life's Journey: what it is, where it can be found, how it can be experienced and the joy and fulfillment that ensues, even in the presence of your adversities.

Part I

The Call

A new beginning and a new ending can be yours today

THERE COMES THAT POINT in your life when all your past mistakes and failures, all your cares and worries, all your sins and shortcomings, all your emptiness and longings - all that defiles and degrades you - can be displaced. They can be completely wiped out from your life and you are given the opportunity to move on freely, immaculate and fully charged as though they never existed. Today can be that day for you. The choice is yours.

Introduction

True Joy and Fulfillment

LIKE THE AVERAGE PERSON, you may at times experience unmet longings; perhaps, even lingering emptiness and hurt that seems to have no cure. They are dormant on pleasant occasions only to later rear their insidious heads.

In an effort to find lasting joy and fulfillment, I could advise you on how to bury your deep rooted pains and insufficiencies with a pleasant smile and a good attitude. However, that's like directing you to put a band-aid on a bleeding, decaying ulcer.

So then, I might say, "try something new; find a hobby". Yet, after the activities have ceased, in the still of the night, remains that hunger for something more. So, maybe I could advise you on how to chase after your dreams in pursuit of joy and fulfillment. But, the reality is, you may very well accomplish those dreams, and be left miserable, empty and unfulfilled.

It's good to maintain a pleasant outward demeanor and a positive attitude; do the activities you enjoy and strive towards your temporal goals. However, these should not be perceived as the quick-fix method towards lifelong joy and fulfillment. They cannot suffice.

The pursuit of these targets neither paves the road towards a joyful and fulfilling life nor is their accomplishment the beginning of one. They can only guarantee moments of highs within a lifetime of lows. Therefore, in taking this route, you will only be led to fill your life with pleasant adventures that can offer the highs so as to distract yourself from the reality of the lows. This will not solve the problem. Yet, this is exactly what most of us have been cultured to do from we entered into this world.

We were cultured to seek after the goals, events and lifestyle that make us happy. However, this good feeling of happiness is very superficial and transient. It lasts only as long as we do what we enjoy and attain what we want out of life.

But we don't always get to do all the things we would enjoy and achieve exactly what we want out of life. Other times, even when we do the activities we enjoy and achieve what we want, we find that instead of finding lasting contentment, we want more. That's because we have a natural desire for a deeper level of contentment that cannot be adequately satisfied by activities and the accomplishment of worldly pursuits. In addition, with this approach, when some aspects of our life would appear to be flourishing, other essential aspects such as our spirituality might be enduring apparent dearth.

The word happiness is often used interchangeably with joy. However, one school of thought views happiness as a sense of contentment that is derived from pleasurable circumstances and experiences. But, *joy is viewed as a deeper level, in fact the very deepest level of contentment; it comes from within and is not dictated by external circumstances or external factors.*

Our life can be compared to a cup of tea. Without a sweetener it's bland and less enjoyable. We have 2 choices of sweeteners: an artificial sweetener and real sugar. Artificial sweeteners taste like real sugar but do not provide the nutrients of sugar. This is good for us because we tend to over-consume sugar; but, let's say we weren't consuming sugar at all and were using an artificial sweetener to completely replace all of our sugar needs. Though we enjoy the taste of the artificial sweetener, wouldn't we at some point feel the impact of using it to substitute all our sugar needs since it cannot provide us the same nutrients of real sugar that our bodies need in its correct proportion?

An artificial sweetener can be compared to the happiness that is created by our good circumstances in life. As artificial sweeteners provide pleasure for our taste-buds, so do our good circumstances provide happiness to our lives. Nothing is wrong with this. But there is something that they cannot provide. Just like when an artificial sweetener is used to completely substitute real sugar it will leave a nutritional void, the same applies when happiness is used to substitute true joy. Something will be missing from our lives. We might not notice immediately or be able to pinpoint it but a void would still be there.

As a result of the good feeling we get, this *happiness* that comes from the pleasurable things and experiences of life can be easily confused with lasting joy. Therefore, our natural appetite for true joy can be delusively quenched and diverted towards fulfillment from the things of this life that make us happy.

Quite often, these things are influenced by our desire for: affluence, pleasure, and admiration. But there are many people who will accomplish these, plus more, yet still complain of a daunting reality of emptiness. That's because we can never find real joy and wholesome satisfaction from a life that is aimed at merely serving and gratifying self.

Reflect carefully on your own earthly goals and desires. These may not be all bad; they may include family, education, career, good health which are not bad in and of themselves. Think also of why you ultimately desire these for your life? For the average person, their earthly goals and desires in life ultimately lead towards one hope: experiencing joy and fulfillment in life. Our temporal goals and desires, though we might not readily notice, are usually our means of getting to this end.

The 2 most frequent mistakes often made in our quest for joy and fulfillment are:

1. We pursue them as the ultimate goal
2. We pursue them through creating and achieving pleasant circumstances, experiences and life objectives

Our pursuit after joy and fulfillment as an ultimate goal is quite understandable. As humans we have an undeniable, natural tendency to seek after joy and fulfillment in life because in the absence of joy and fulfillment is an undesirable void of dullness. For many, this void can be accurately described as sadness and emptiness.

For this reason, even before we recognize it, we are cultured to seek after joy and fulfillment through the pursuit of certain earthly goals and desires, whose accomplishments will make us feel good. The intricacies of this pursuit may vary somewhat from one culture to another and from one era to another but the route is always through attaining earthly accomplishments. But in reality this only leads to happiness and not true joy.

If our desirable possessions, circumstances and experiences are removed, then this will be the proof of the matter – this is the deciding factor of whether or not we have real joy or only superficial happiness.

Reflect on your own life:

- Are you truly a *joyful person* living the *joyful life*?
- What is your source of joy?
- Where are you looking to find joy?
- If your possessions, pleasant circumstances and experiences are removed – will you be able to honestly say that you are still a joyful person and still living a joyful life?
- Could it be that there is a higher level of contentment that you are missing out on?

After having a heavy meal, we know when we're filled. We're not left in doubt as to whether we've had enough to eat. The same is true for fulfillment in life. *Fulfillment comes with the sense of having our lives saturated with all that gives life true meaning, purpose and value.*

Among the greatest accounts of finding true joy and fulfillment in life, is recorded in the life sketches of a man who attained joy in the presence of seemingly nothing but miserable circumstances. He lost his reputation, his standing in society; he was beaten, repeatedly imprisoned, and his life was threatened. Yet he attests to finding the greatest riches of life, not when he had the abundance of temporal riches of this life but, after he lost those and, attained that which truly matters in life. This man is the apostle Paul; (2 Corinthians 11:23 & Philippians 3:7 & 8).

His predicament could not rob him of his joy. Being imprisoned did not bar him from living life to the fullest invested in him; because, experiencing the fullness of joy and absolute fulfillment in life is not defined by our circumstances.

Even today we can read the accounts of Paul's life that bear testimony of His profound joy. The depth and breadth of his quality of life are still evidenced by the undying epistles of Ephesians, Philippians, Colossians and Philemon which he wrote while in prison. Yet how many of us have pleasant circumstances in life but have not joy; are free to live but powerless to live life to its fullest?

What then makes for the joyful and fulfilling life?

This is a question that is pondered by all of us at some point: from the poor to the rich and from the ordinary to the greatest minds. The importance of joy and fulfillment to our lives has inspired many to look deeply into the issue; but, how many of us have really unraveled and claimed the solution? How many have truly claimed that life of never-ending joy and fulfillment?

Yet the answer to this innate longing, our lifelong quest, is well within the grasp of every single human being. There are many roads that lead to happiness, but only one Road offers true joy and fulfillment in life. This is the Road that you are now being invited to Journey, wholeheartedly, on. As you journey, this will most likely be your serendipity - you would have discovered far more than that which you set out to find.

Experiencing the Essence of Life's Journey

Have you ever had a food craving where you're not quite able to put your finger on the exact food that would fill that craving? You reach for a food item to satisfy the craving but after you've eaten it, the craving is still there. You sense the desire for something more. The same is true of our unmet craving for joy and fulfillment in life.

We've all experienced this void; but many of us have never accurately deduced what really is this longing, what is needed to fill it or how to go about having it filled. We often seek to fill it, but only from seeking after the wrong things and looking in the wrong places.

As for the average person, even with enormous worldly accomplishments, the more of this world he has, the more he seeks after in an attempt to find satisfaction; but never coming to the point where he is truly satisfied. That's because these things cannot furnish us with exactly what is required to fulfill this innate craving. There will always remain an empty space - and consequently, an appetite, a craving to fill that void.

As we've seen so far, this void cannot be filled by any or even a combination of the greatest temporal allurements that this world can offer. This accounts for the reason this void is obvious in the life of not only the unaccomplished but also the life of many so-called accomplished individuals or even celebrities who seem to have it all. Yet they resort to addictions and sometimes even suicide as an escape from this reality of emptiness amidst their seeming success.

That is the great danger of pursuing after the things of this world to find joy and fulfillment. Such pursuit is not only inadequate to fill this innate void, and it doesn't only barricade us from finding the real solution, but its accomplishments may also result in lingering feelings of excruciating disappointment and regrets. Therefore, any person who has gained great worldly accomplishments while still experiencing this void naturally suffers from frustration and feelings that life is not worth living. But life is worth living!

Life is worth living, not because of great worldly achievements but, when we have found, accepted and experienced God Himself and allow Him to recreate us, and fuel and direct our lives. This happens only as we surrender to the sovereignty of God. That place, that void, was intentionally reserved in our hearts and lives to be occupied by God. It can only be suitably filled by God Himself. He is the Fountain of Life from which flows the very essence of our lives.

God is the Source of the Essence of Life's Journey.

So, what then is this Essence of Life's Journey? It is all that is needed to live the joyful and fulfilling life. It includes and surpasses true joy and absolute fulfillment in life. It is experienced when we are spiritually nourished by the Fountain of Life. This is the only assurance of experiencing the very best of life. In this experience is found the abundant life.

Experiencing the Essence of Life's Journey is having the Holy Spirit of God recreating us, fueling and steering our lives, and journeying with us. When this happens, everything of real significance to life falls right into place.

Contrary to how we have been cultured to believe, joy and fulfillment in life are not goals within themselves. They are by-products of a rich relationship with the Source Himself. As we look deeper into this topic it will become increasingly obvious why any pursuit where joy and fulfillment is made to be the end or the goal of the pursuit will only leave us disappointed. God must become this goal before we can ever truly find lasting joy and fulfillment.

You experience the Essence of Life's Journey when you become the temple of the Holy Ghost. God doesn't just want to lavish the things of this world into your life. He doesn't just desire to lavish spiritual blessings on you either. He wants to fill you with Himself. You were created for that. You were deliberately created with that capacity.

God yearns to unlock the door to wholly fill that space in your life. He wants to reposition you. He wants to live in your heart; change your heart, your values, your path, your entire life. God desires to recreate you first and foremost so that He can empower you to live the joyful and fulfilling life that He designed for you to live.

We all need God. We were born with this unmet need. Deep down inside, we all have an innate longing for this need to be fulfilled. So often in life, we see our need for the qualities and the life that only God can offer without recognizing our even more fundamental need, which is our need for God Himself. We are all aware that we crave the joyful and fulfilling life. But often, what many of us do not realize is that what we truly crave is God – who is embodied by this joyful and fulfilling life – the solution to filling that void of dullness and emptiness.

It's like being in a hot desert where you recognize your thirst, and the need for this thirst to be quenched. But you must also come to that point where you recognize and acknowledge that water is the only source that can adequately quench your thirst, before you will seek after the water in order for your thirst to be quenched. A dull life, or even sadness and emptiness that confront us in this world, help us to realize our need for joy and fulfillment in life. Yet, unless we recognize, acknowledge and seek after the true Source, we can never be filled.

As with our thirst for water, this innate void that we all experience is not completely a bad thing. It's like an alarm indicating to us that a fundamental need is unmet in our lives and propelling us towards having it filled. God allows it this way as a means of helping us to recognize our need for Him and what only Him can offer to our lives.

Feelings of gloominess and emptiness are merely symptoms of our unmet need for God. Though this might be received as disturbing news, these lingering feelings of discontentment actually point to the state of our relationship with God. They indicate that we either are not journeying with God or we have not truly surrendered all and are journeying in a close enough relationship with Him for this void to be filled.

For many reasons, some of us are more prone to experiencing these symptoms than others. But we all do, even at one point or another during our lifetime. The solution comes only in finding comfort in God and in seeking for a deeper, richer relationship with Him. The solution comes with faith in God and what He can accomplish in you and through you. God wants to replace your longings and all your negative feelings with His presence so that you can rise with newness of life.

If you feel the need to live a better life, fundamentally, what you need is God and more of Him. He offers the remedy for all of life's challenges and concerns. He is the remedy for your unfulfilled needs and longings – even your need for true joy and absolute fulfillment in life.

Without God dwelling in you and taking control of the reigns of your life, you can never be complete. There would always remain that void - that longing and emptiness. This applies to your life, regardless of how successful you are in your endeavors. Our circumstances in life can easily deceive us. Some of us may be at that point in life where we feel we can have it all outside of God's rich presence in our lives.

But, if we go searching for the genuine joyful and fulfilling life, separate and apart from God, we can never find it. Life has true meaning, purpose and value only when God is present: recreating us, redirecting and fueling our lives.

If your life ever feels like an old rusting car that's parked up in a junk yard then you'll understand exactly what God needs to accomplish in you in order to bestow on you the life He desires for you to live. That car must first be repaired or recreated to be fit for the road. It must also be appropriately fuelled with the right stuff to be equipped for the journey. Then it must be properly driven by a capable driver in order to effectively cover its journey. All this now creates new meaning, purpose and value to the existence of that car.

God has given us freely of the Holy Spirit in order to *recreate* us to be the persons He desires for us to be and therefore equipping us to live the life that He designed for us to live. But like gasoline to a car, our lives also need to be constantly replenished as we journey throughout life. Through the Holy Spirit, our lives are *fuelled* with all the positive emotions, energy, principles and motivation to live life at its best, as God desires for all of us. The Holy Spirit also *drives* us by empowering us to make the right decisions so that we can journey throughout life, attaining the goals that God designed for our lives.

Fundamentally, the Spirit of God in you works in your life to:
- Convict and save you (John 16:7&8; 2 Thessalonians 2:13)
- Renew and empower you (Romans 8:11)
- Mold you spiritually towards perfection / towards cultivating the pure Fruit of the Spirit (1 Corinthians 6:11; Galatians 5:22&23)

- Impart spiritual gift(s); such as: teaching, healing, prophesying, etc. to enable you to effectively perform God's Will (Ephesians 4:11-13)
- Teach and forewarn you (John 14:26;16:13)

The measure of the life you live is determined by the limit you place on the reigning presence and power of God in your life. Living abundantly therefore equates to being utterly filled and controlled by God's Holy Spirit. This is when you will accurately experience in its fullness, the Essence of Life's Journey.

You cannot create true joy and lasting fulfillment for yourself in life. Though we try very hard to convince ourselves otherwise, as mere humans, we do not have this level of power over life, even our own lives. You cannot obtain true joy and lasting fulfillment through activities either. This life ensues from something greater. It ensues from a deep, rich relationship with God. Your answer therefore lies in not only discovering this Source but seeking to journey with God intimately.

Chapter 1

Exploring A New Journey

Life's Journey

LIFE IS NOT JUST a series of events. It's a Journey. Figuratively, in life's Journey, there are always two roads ahead of us: the Broad Road and the Narrow Road (Matthew 7:13&14). In fact, you are already on one of them.

There is the Broad Road that is paved with temporal pleasures, eternal hurt and emptiness. God does not inhabit there; religion maybe, but not God. Many of us make our way on this Road, especially in pursuit of joy and fulfillment; often without even making a conscious effort to journey there. That's because this road promises to lead to the fulfillment of many of our temporal goals and desires. But, unfortunately, even this promise is not guaranteed. This road seems right yet, in actual fact, it only paves the way that ends with destruction (Proverbs 14:12).

On the other hand, the Narrow Road offers: love, joy, peace, perseverance and the abiding presence of God, even in the midst of adversities. The Narrow Road is the Way, which cultivates perpetual unadulterated joy. In it is the fulfilling, abundant life. All these, the Broad Road can never offer, despite its seasonal pleasures. The Narrow Road is *the only Way* through which perpetual, lifelong joy and fulfillment ensues. It is said to be narrow because it is bordered by the principles of true godliness, and so only few manage to journey there.

The Broad Road represents the direction of that person whose life is un-surrendered to God. On the other hand, the Narrow Road represents the direction embarked on by the life surrendered to God. The Narrow Road can be entered only through faith in Christ Jesus.

That's because Christ is this Narrow Road. Entering onto this Road symbolizes entering into the life of Christ, through faith. This means accepting Christ for who he is and what he is offering you. This includes a willingness to let go of all that you now have and seek to have, in exchange for all that he's offering you. We can never truly experience the richness of the joy and fulfillment that God desires to bless us with until we have first come to that place where we are willing to submit our entire lives to Him; that is allowing Him to govern our lives, through Jesus Christ. This leads, not just to the best life now on earth but also to eternal life.

It's impossible to speak about experiencing the abundant life today on earth without speaking about eternal life. It is the same Life-giver who empowers us to live a fulfilling life here and now that qualifies us to live eternally. The abundant life is not merely a life of joy and fulfillment on this present earth. When we step into this life that Christ is offering us today, we step into that eternal life also.

Interestingly, we all started our journey on the Broad Road and have all existed on it for some time. Yet, only those who have dared to cross over to the Narrow Road and journeyed there, have truly lived. Only those who have dared to give up their self-made and self-directed life for the life that Christ offers would have truly experienced the abundant life. This is where it all begins. It starts with that decision to transition from our own self-seeking path in life to the Path that has been designed for us in Christ.

God has a unique plan for all of us. By choosing to embark on the Journey of the joyful and fulfilling life you must faithfully voyage on the Narrow Road in a unique *lane* that your Lord has designated for you as an individual. In all of earth's history, your distinct lane will never be travelled by anyone but you. It is the life that God has designed for you. It is marked by God's distinct Plan for your life, which also incorporates your personality, circumstances, experiences and background.

Just like God had a distinct plan for Moses, Joseph, Abraham, Paul and those other persons mentioned in the Bible, He also has a distinct plan for you. How then will you be able to make the right steps - the right decisions – along the way? You have a personal Guide to direct you every single step of the way. All that you're required to do is to willingly and obediently follow.

Your Guide

As a child I've always heard the cliché "Jesus is the answer", yet never fully appreciated the value of this truth until I've experienced it myself. Jesus is the answer to all of life's questions and conflicts.

He is our Savior (Acts 4:12). He is not one of many saviors - he is the only Savior. There is no other. So, to be restored into fellowship with God the Father, we must accept His Son Jesus Christ (1Timothy 2:5 & John 14:6).

He is the Truth; he is the Life and he is the Way (St John 14:6). All the truth of this universe and our existence is wrapped up in Christ (Colossians 1:12-19). In him dwells the fullness of God which is made available to us. You are complete in Christ (Colossians 2:8-10). All your emptiness and void begin to be filled when you have found yourself in Christ.

That's because he is the Narrow Road - that Way to the Father. In Christ you cannot be lost because he is the Way itself. He is the Road, which the Father has provided to Himself, to the best life on this present earth and the Road to everlasting life. Christ is the Way to the life that was designed for you to live, starting even today.

Yet, Christ is Life itself. Christ offers life and life even more abundantly (John 10:10).Regardless of how messed-up, lifeless, purposeless and broken we might feel in this world, rejuvenating life can be found in Christ by all of us. Through him, and through him only, can be experienced the Essence of Life's Journey which equips us to live the joyful and fulfilling life now and to live eternally. What better guide to have than this!

Have you found the Messiah? Have you found your life Source, your Savior, your Guide, your Path? When you have, your heart will be at peace. Your lifelong reason for being here will be fulfilling and, despite your circumstances, you will be experiencing the joy associated with living life at its best.

This joy is not a result of pleasant circumstances, worldly possessions, scholarly attainment or promising successes. It's a consequence of you obtaining something higher; something more glorious; something that cannot be bought or sold, cannot be tarnished by disasters or weathered by time. You would have found the Life-giver and the Life-giver has granted you another chance to experience the power of God recreating you, and redirecting and replenishing your life.

Who is Jesus Christ to you?

Take time to think about Jesus and what he means to you personally. Reflect on the impact you have allowed him to have in your life. You may be a very dedicated member of a church and live in perfect accordance with the letter of the Law, but reflect on whether you are truly following Christ. Is he Lord of your life? Is he in charge? Or are you and your personal opinions and desires directing your life?

This is the distinguishing factor between Christians, true followers of Christ, and every other individual. True followers have accepted that invitation to have Christ live in their hearts and, through the indwelling of the Holy Spirit, guide their entire lives. Their Path is paved and directed by him. They are truly *followers*; they're not *the guide* for *their own path*. They have embarked on an intimate companionship with their Lord and Savior.

Like every relationship, it takes time to get to know your Heavenly Father and His Son Jesus Christ. It is through this relationship; however, that God practically imparts abundant, eternal life (John 17:3). This is because, through your intimate knowledge of and experience with God, you would be consciously guided through your temporary Journey, right into eternity.

If you haven't done so already, take that time to become acquainted with your Guide. You must! It will be worth it. Those precious moments will become the turning point – the most priceless and significant moments of your entire life. If you haven't fully accepted God's Calling, those moments with Him will further prepare you to wholly embrace it. God is calling you, even now, to walk with Him in an amazing new Journey.

The Call

Most of us, at some point, have made an application for a position, a job offer, then sit around and wait anxiously for that interview call or that call to notify us that we've been accepted. Unfortunately, for many, that call never came; mainly because a number of applicants vie for a single coveted vacancy. Only the very best of all the applicants will eventually be called - or at least, the one who proves himself to be the best. This therefore requires a great deal of effort, competitiveness and outstanding attributes to impress and win the favor of the assessor.

Do we often have the illusion that a similar situation exists with God - our Divine Assessor? The Good News is: every single individual, including you, has been called by God even before any of us realize this Calling or acknowledge our need for what God is offering.

Before you were conceived in the womb, God knew you (Jeremiah 1:5). Before you were known to anyone on earth, including your parents, the Ruler of the universe knew you. You are a product of not merely your parents, but the very mind and handy work of the Creator Himself. He thought of you before you came into being. His thoughts extended beyond your unique personal features to a special slot, just for you, in this life and the next.

There is a place for you in Christ - a special lane for you on the Narrow Road and this leads to your special place in the life to come. This vacancy, in this life and in eternity, was prepared just for you and can only be filled by you. Neglecting to accept this Call will result in your slot being eternally vacant. By neglecting to fully respond to this call you can never enter into the joy of the Lord and the fulfilling life that is found only in Him.

You don't have to impress God or compete for this slot. It was designed for you. It is already yours upon your acceptance of it. God is granting you a new beginning, right now. It is not God who needs to accept you, but you who need to accept Him and what He has already prepared and is offering you. This Call is your ticket to the great riches of life. Have you answered the Call? Is your divinely ordained post still vacant?

What is this Call?

The knowledge of your past helps you to understand where you currently are. Where you're coming from, helps you to also appreciate where you're destined towards. All this affords you a sense of direction. In journeying ahead, it's therefore imperative to have a clear understanding of where you are coming from. Let's therefore reflect on where it all started.

God created the sinless couple in the Garden of Eden to share in an intimate relationship with Him, reflect His image and carry out His Will (Genesis 1&2). Adam and Eve had uninterrupted communion with their Maker. They were one with God - one in purpose, one in desire, one in Spirit. They shared an intimate spiritual connection with their God.

They were *perfect* in all respect. They had a beautiful, flawless garden as their home. They had each other. Most importantly, they had in its fullness the undiluted richness of the presence of God Himself nourishing their lives. God provided them all that they needed to live the joyful and fulfilling life.

God envisioned all this to be exploited by future generations as well. However, the devil also had his own plans for the couple and subsequent generations.

When the devil convinced Eve that God has withheld from them that which would improve their already perfect image, she chose to exchange the presence of her Creator for the false notion of self-exaltation (Genesis 3:1-6). So often we see sin only in the context of breaking 1 of the 10 commandments, as is spelt out in the Law. But sin goes beyond the mere letters of the Law. Living with little or no regard for the sovereignty of God over our lives is sinful. A person living a self-governed, self-centered life and appears to be keeping all 10 commandments is no less disobedient to God as the liar or the thief.

The principle of sin is clearly demonstrated in Adam and Eve's disobedience. Adam and Eve gave up the very essence of their being in pursuing after their self-seeking venture – they gave up God. They turned their backs on God when they relinquished His sovereignty over their lives. Significantly, that instant, for the first time, humanity experienced sadness and emptiness. Through disobedience, they chose to walk away from the Will of God. With that decision, they lost it all.

They lost their connection with God and everything associated with His presence. They lost the garden. That very instant they lost the great riches of their lives. The image they aimed at exalting, merely deteriorated. They stepped away from their rightful slot in life. They stepped away from the Narrow Road onto the Broad Road and automatically repositioned themselves and humanity. They stepped away from light and walked into darkness. By walking away from the Source of life, they exchanged eternal and spiritual life for eternal and spiritual death.

By doing this, they not only forfeited God's Plan for their own lives, but also His Plan for subsequent generations - His Plan for your life included. For this reason, you were born on the Broad Road. Though not by design, you were therefore born detached from your Maker.

Regardless of how beautiful and masterfully crafted a lamp is, this amounts to no great significance unless the lamp is powered and enabled to perform as it was designed to. The lamp was designed to offer light; but unless it is connected to the power source the true meaning, value and purpose of its existence can never be realized. The same applies to our lives too.

The Bible often uses oil to represent the work of the Holy Spirit in empowering our lives (1 Samuel 16:13 & Matthew 25:1-13). We are like lamps and the Holy Spirit is like the oil. If we consider this in the context of our society today, the Holy Spirit to our lives is like electricity to a lamp. The Holy Spirit empowers us to function in the manner that we were created to function.

When disconnected from God, we're therefore merely like lamps without oil or electricity - loaded with potential yet useless without the power source. Like the disconnected lamp, such existence is purposeless, the lives futile and unfulfilling. This explains why even our best attempt to living the joyful and fulfilling life in that disconnected state will only prove to be pointless.

But, all hope was not lost in the Garden of Eden. Our loving Father devised a plan to reposition humanity: to restore you to your ordained slot. What was lost in one garden was conquered in another. Through Jesus Christ's death in the Garden of Gethsemane, God opened up the Way for us to be restored to the slot we were created to occupy. The Way was opened for us to once more be connected with the Source of our being; to live the joyful and fulfilling life, right here and now, and to live eternally.

Once more, the opportunity is available for us to reflect God's character; to be bearers of His Light. God made a Way and has extended an invitation for us to accept it. He is calling all of us to repent and return to our position, our individual lane, on the Narrow Road of life.

God is calling you to a new beginning: to become a new person and to live a new life. This is the entrance to the joyful, fulfilling life we all desire. This invitation can only be responded to at the individual level. No one can respond to another person's Call. This Call is a personal invitation to claim what is rightfully yours through Christ Jesus.

Picture a situation where a prince left his father's throne and all the luxuries of royalty. He lived as a pauper and died as a criminal for the sake of redeeming a sibling who blindly chose the life of a pauper instead of a royalty. Yet after this sacrifice has been made, the sibling refused to accept it. He chose instead to continue on his merry, or more accurately, self-destructive path. Isn't that what we do when we ignore what Christ has done on our behalf?

The devil convinced Eve into believing that the Broad Road was more self-exalting, more rewarding and fulfilling. Yet it proved otherwise - only after it was already too late. Today, the devil is doing the same to encourage us to remain on that Road that our fore-parents have blindly chosen. Today we have the examples of Adam and Eve's wrong decision to learn from. We therefore should not be buying that same lie.

Adam and Eve lost the great splendors of this life in setting out on their self-governed, self-seeking venture. Why do we believe we can regain the best of this life by pursuing a similar venture? To the contrary, our only hope of reclaiming that better life is to terminate that very blunder that started with Adam and Eve and has continued with our own lives.

Through Christ's death, he opened the way for us to be restored into the life that God designed for us to live. Through his life, he declared that it is indeed possible for the redeemed person to be one with God and live in accordance with God's Will, even in this sin infested world.

Christ is offering you a new heart and a new life, even a joyful and fulfilling life. This genuine new life can be found only in Christ Jesus, not a particular church, not in patterning a religious life, not from any organization, not from a mere human being - but through a divine being. It can be found only through Christ, who is the Way and the Life.

Look for example at the life of Saul. Saul was on his own journey, making his own decisions, living His own life, with his own goals and his own desires. Unfortunately, he thought his way was consistent with God's. But, while attending to his mission to persecute Christians, Saul was suddenly stopped in his tracks by the spectacular appearance of the risen Savior himself.

With trembling and astonishment Saul's question to Christ was: "Lord, what will you have me do?" In that instant Saul surrendered to Christ and allowed Christ to change him and his life. Christ converted Saul, redirected his life and replenished it with the Spirit of love. Saul was converted from being a foe of Christ to becoming a friend, even a follower. His mission was changed from persecuting Christians to spreading the gospel of Jesus Christ. (Acts 9:1-31)

God's Calling is to recreate us and to redirect and replenish our lives - He desires to reform our character and consequently, our lives. He has to do this before we can ever experience His joy and find fulfillment through Him. God called us from one position to another and for a specific purpose. We are called (1 Peter 2:9):

- from darkness to light (or more literally from being sinful to becoming righteous; from living a self-governed life to living in accordance with God's Will)
- for the purpose of glorifying God, and
- to be identified among His royal priesthood/holy nation (or God's spiritual community of believers)

Accepting this Call leads you to become the person God desires for you to be and to fulfill His ordained Plan for your life. It is a Call to journey in that spiritual lane that God designed for you.

Accepting God's Call begins a genuine transformation to becoming royalty: a son or daughter of the God of Heaven. As John exclaims: "How great is the love the Father has lavished on us, that we should be called children of God" (1 John 3:1). Such matchless, unconditional love is beyond our comprehension. Yet it is real. It is being extended to you, even now. Knowing this is important, but responding to it, is of even greater significance.

God calls all of us to a higher and nobler life. This great Call can be likened to a two-phase Master Plan. That is, a Call to:

1. Salvation from sin (and it's consequence of eternal death and separation from God)

2. Empowerment to live above sin and in accordance with God's Will for our lives on earth (Sanctification)

Many Christians have experienced the great power of salvation (Step 1) but are hesitant in journeying from there towards sanctification (step 2). Like unbelievers, some of us have never truly strived to experience the fullness of that second phase of the Master Plan that God designed for us to exploit on this earth.

We've not allowed God to thoroughly fill that void. After being saved, we've endeavored to endure life on the Narrow Road as we journey but, have never really exploited the heights of the bliss of that life in Christ. Such lives, though redirected from the Broad Road onto the Narrow Road, remain un-replenished. This is because we would not have truly surrendered all, including our fears and insecurities, and trusted God to renew our entire life.

Unless we trust God for this empowerment, we will miss out on experiencing the fullness of God's Plan for our lives, after we have been saved. God wants you to become both saved and sanctified. This is the only way you can truly enter into the joy and fulfillment that God designed for your new life.

Just as salvation is claimed through faith, living the ordained life of the saved comes by claiming it through faith. It comes through an acceptance of God's Great Plan in totality and by allowing its fulfillment throughout our lives as we journey.

This 2nd phase of the Master Plan comes with abiding in Christ. It involves:

- an intimate connection with God
- character development and transformation
- becoming God's ambassador on earth
- serving God wholeheartedly and being of service to others as God ordains it
- understanding and fulfilling God's unique purpose for your life as you journey throughout this life

God is always communicating His Will for our lives to us, but how slow we are in understanding His speech. So often, we are too occupied in our own pursuits to even recognize His directives. Most times, it is only when God shouts at us, through allowing extreme situations, that we are brought to the place where we recognize His voice. For this reason, God used a burning bush that was not consumed by the fire to attract Moses' attention to Him and His Will for Moses' life (Exodus 3:2). What might God be using to call your attention to Him and His Will for your life?

Would God Really Call Me?

You might find yourself in a certain situation or place in life and wonder how you got there. You may not even know how to find your way out. But God knows exactly where you are, the circumstances that surround you and precisely how to rescue you. Never can you become so sinful, so wretched, or sink so emotionally low where you fall below the depth which your Savior's powerful and loving hands can grasp and lift you up to His Standard.

Neither can you become so lofty to surpass the majesty of God Himself and that which He has to offer you. No matter how bountiful your worldly attainment, it cannot match or exceed what God has in store for you. He desires for you to explore His awesome presence and exploit His blessings. Regardless of your circumstances, you are within the capacity of God's reach and His Will.

When we make decisions that separate us from God's guidance, we often feel this also separates us from His love for us. God hates sin. We will no doubt experience His wrath towards sin when we choose to embrace sin in our hearts and lives. But we must also be reminded that God loves us unconditionally – that is, even beyond our sinfulness. When we are separated from God by sin, His heart wanders after us. He yearns to rescue us from our destructive life so that we can find rest in His presence.

Whether or not we are aware of this, our absence in God's fold is felt. God has a special place and a special task for you, which is left vacant and undone when you're absent from the complete realm of His Master Plan. No matter how insignificant you may feel on this earth or in God's Plan, this is contrary to God's feelings and attitude towards you.

The parable is told by Christ of a single sheep, out of 100, that wandered from the fold (Luke 15:1-7). The Master was never at peace until after diligently searching for that one sheep, He found him and restored him to the fold. Oh, what a rejoicing that was! He called His friends to celebrate with Him because His sheep that was lost is now found.

That's the amount of energy, attention, emotion God extends toward any of His children who wanders from His guiding presence. When the sheep was found, there was rejoicing because at that point, what really mattered was not that the sheep strayed, but that he has been found.

God's major concern is not your past mistakes or misdeeds. God is concerned about the decision you are making right now, this moment. The real issue is about the choice you will consciously make today, concerning the person you will be and the quality of life you will live, starting this moment.

Upon repentance, as far as the east is from the west, is as far as God separates your sin from you (Psalm 103:12). It must not interfere with the deep connection He wants to establish with you. It must not interfere with the absolute fulfillment and joy He desires for you to experience in His presence.

God has been calling you. He has a great Plan for you. Maybe you've never recognized this great truth before but, like the lost sheep, God hasn't only been calling you; He has been pursuing after you. He wants you. And He's determined to claim you as His precious child. He longs for you to experience His love and His goodness towards you.

Every person is precious in God's sight. You are precious in His sight. Had He not loved you unconditionally and appreciated your worth, you would not be here in the first place. When He thought of you, He also thought you were worth the while. You may be thinking, "Not me - I'm an accident. I wasn't planned for. I can't possibly be in God's special Plan"; but not so. The circumstances under which you were conceived by your parents might have been unplanned and accidental on their part but that doesn't make your existence an accident on God's part.

Genesis 38 gives the interesting background to Pharez's birth. Judah, married a Canaanite woman and produced, at the time of interest, 3 sons through this union. The first son was wicked so when Judah found him a wife, God killed him. The second son refused to impregnate the eldest brother's widow who was handed down to him in wedlock, so God became angry and killed him too.

Judah promised the widow his third son for a husband as soon as the son was grown, but did not keep this promise. The widow, being very determined, deceptively played the role of a prostitute with Judah and became pregnant. Through prostitution, Pharez was conceived. Yet even more significant than the manner in which he was conceived, was the divine Plan God had for his life.

Pharez was chosen during his generation to be the one to continue the lineage that led to Christ. He became 5th in line in the genealogy of Abraham that continued unto Christ. What an honor and awesome privilege! Pharez's life meant so much to God that God became angry at

Judah's second son when he refused to impregnate his wife, thus preventing Pharez's birth. That's how much even your existence means to God. That's how much His Will for your life matters to Him.

How do you fit into God's Plan? This should be your greatest concern. Yet, this you can never fully grasp unless you have endeavored to journey on the Narrow Road. Have you started that Journey?

Have I Responded to the Call?

If you literally step out of utter darkness and walk into a poorly lit area, the lighting of the latter can be very comforting in comparison to being in the complete dark. The fact that it's a little brighter conditions your mind to soon appreciate this state as if it was fully lit; especially if you can help yourself around without stumbling too much.

On leaving a well lit room and entering a poorly lit room, the difference can be startling. However, after remaining in that poorly lit room for some time, your eyes become adjusted to the lighting. Before long you will forget the darkness in the room. The darkness is no longer noticeable. But, it's still there.

Your spiritual life is similar. Remaining in the same condition over a period of time can train your eyes to appreciate that state. This can happen even when the presence of something as essential as Light, the guiding presence of God, is missing or diminished. God does not offer you semi-light or darkness. He desires for you to walk in the fullness of light so that you can live abundantly, in accordance with His Will.

The truth is, WE HAVE ALL RESPONDED TO GOD'S CALL. By remaining passive we automatically reject our Call. Actively, we choose to respond by either out-rightly accepting or rejecting this Call. We *cannot* accept this Call and remain passive. A half-hearted, one-foot-in and one foot-out response is also no better than rejecting this Call completely. So then, how do you know for certain if you have genuinely accepted this Call?

Self-examination

Socrates, the notable Greek philosopher, was placed on trial for his public discussions on issues related to the examination of great truths about life, including true virtue in the life of a person. These, he considered as essential issues of life; however, his conclusions on these issues contradicted the lifestyle of prominent public figures and the traditional knowledge of his time and society. The jury granted him the opportunity to either remain silent with his reasoning or die.

Socrates retorted, "The unexamined life is not worth living!" For Socrates, life had no value, unless truths about essential issues of life are unraveled and embraced through deep consideration. It is believed that he chose the death penalty above the unexamined life.

In modern society, we do not have to choose between a death penalty and an examined life. But, could it be that in choosing not to examine our own lives, we unconsciously choose some form of death penalty above self-examination? Could it be that we automatically choose spiritual and eternal death?

What is the real significance of self-examination? Why would Socrates consider the examined life to be worthy of attention to the point of paying so great a price?

Self-examination reveals the reality of where we stand. Without self-examination we can be stagnant and never even know it. Though mobile, we may be in a circular motion or moving backwards in our principles and life goals while being ignorant to this fact. Without self-examination, we may think we are at a certain altitude, when in reality we are not. Most importantly, we may fall miserably below God's standard for our lives without ever being conscious of this.

Self-examination reveals where you are in the sphere of God's Master Plan for your life. It reveals 'where you are' spiritually in comparison to:

- where you started out, and
- where you ought to be

You started out in spiritual darkness (sin) and should be advancing in spiritual light (righteousness).

We already have a clear picture of: where we are coming from and where we ought to be heading - where God has called us from and where He intends for us to be. The question then is: "Where am I now?" It is time for deep reflection. Take some time to examine your own life. Reflect on the following:

1. Where has God called me from?
2. Where has God called me to?

3. Where am I now?

4. What has God called me for?

5. Is God's Master Plan being fulfilled in my life?

6. Is God being glorified through all aspects of my life?

7. Where is my life practically heading?

Personalize all the questions to suit your unique life. For instance, what specific darkness has God called you out of? Have you merely dropped off a few bad habits, picked up a few good ones and maybe joined a religious group or have you completely abandoned your old self and that old life?

Careful reflection can give a clear indication of whether or not you have completely accepted the Call. As we have seen so far, your response to this Call determines whether you have accepted or rejected Christ's invitation to live life at its best – to live your divinely ordained reason for being on this earth and to live the quality of life God is offering you. Your response to this Call defines whether or not the life that was gifted to you is really being lived and whether the one you are now living is worth continue living.

If you now discover that you have, for one reason or another, rejected this Call, there is no reason for despair. You have the Lord's attention and He's still waiting on your positive response. He is eager to journey with you. He's longing to fill you with Himself. He longs to have you occupy that place on this earth that only you were destined to fill. Are you ready to accept that Call?

Chapter 2

Embarking on Your New Journey

Accepting the Call

In accepting God's Call, we will come to appreciate His amazing grace. This will lead us to repent and confess of our sins, surrender all to Him, and accept all that He offers in return.

Amazing Grace

According to the laws that God gave to Moses to impart to the Israelites, adultery is an offense, punishable by death (Leviticus 20:10). A man and a woman who are caught in adultery should be stoned to death.

One morning, an Israelite woman caught in adultery was brought to Christ, in the absence of her adulterer (John 8:1-11). The character of Christ was being placed on trial by the Scribes and Pharisees who brought her. However, the heart of God towards the unrighteous was ultimately revealed.

When the religious leaders solicited Christ's input in the matter, they were anxious for the opportunity to see him err in his judgment on the issue of justice and mercy. If Christ commanded them to have the adulteress suffer the death penalty, they would have accused him of usurping the Romans' authority; since the Jews were at the time under Roman bondage and were not at liberty to exercise such penalties. If Christ had told them to let her go free, they would also accuse him of breaking the law of God. It was the perfect situation to have Christ cornered.

In order to eradicate sin, such as adultery, from the community, God ordained that the witnesses of the offense should cast the first stones at the accused (Deuteronomy 17:7). By killing each offender of the law, God intended that the community of His people is purified from the presence of sin. But, can evil hands eradicate evil?

"He that is without sin among you, let him first cast a stone at her", proclaimed Christ. Which of the witnesses that caught her in adultery was without sin? None! No one in the audience was without sin, except for Christ. From a guilty conscience, one by one, they all left the company of Christ and the woman, standing alone.

She had no rightful accuser. The only person who was worthy of condemning her, had compassion on her, extended grace towards her and charged her: "Go, and sin no more". Under this condition, grace was extended to her. Instead of being stoned to death, she was given the opportunity to be set free from her death penalty. Her situation is no different from what God is doing for our lives too. This is exactly how God longs to rescue us. This grace is also extended to all of us. We too have also sinned and strayed from God's ideal for our lives.

The adulteress was granted the opportunity to be freed, not only from her death penalty, but also her sinful way. God doesn't just want to remove the penalty and consequences of our destructive life. He wants to remove us from the destructive life itself. God doesn't just desire for us to experience His joy and the fulfillment that He offers. He desires also that the sin problem, our self-centered and self-governed condition, which creates our situation of emptiness and gloom be also removed.

The adulteress's sin was the reason for her death penalty so it must also be removed. With her sin removed, she was no longer condemned to die. She was made worthy to live.

With grace was extended the command: sin no more. The same is extended to us today. To be set free through grace, you must be willing to abandon your old self for the new. To obtain life and life more abundantly, you must first be willing to give up your present life. To fully accept God's grace and His mercies towards you, you must covenant with yourself and with God that you too will sin no more – that you too will no longer allow sin to govern your life, but allow God to take its place.

Confession and Repentance

An offender stood before the judge for the offense of unintentionally killing a boy while operating a motor vehicle under the influence of alcohol. "How do you plea?" asked the judge. "Guilty with explanation", pled the offender.

He then continued to explain that on-going domestic disputes have forced him to resort to alcoholism, leading to the accident and the death of the child. In other words, he wasn't really that guilty after all - or was he?

The verdict was passed: punishment to the fullest extent of the law, with the intention that the offender would realize and acknowledge the magnitude and consequences of his offense. Sounds harsh, doesn't it?

But could it be that this is also our plea to God concerning our sins? There are times when, like that drunk driver, though we're strikingly guilty of an offense, we might never feel the need to be sincerely and completely repentant.

It is true that we have inherited a sinful nature from our fore-parents; but, we've all sinned and fallen below the glory of God (Romans 3:23). The drunkard chose alcoholism; however, alternative provisions, such as counseling, were available options for him to address his domestic issues. A provision is also available for all of us today to address our dispute with God. We have no justifiable excuse.

You might not intentionally rebel against God and His Will for your life but, if your life does not conform to His government, then you are no doubt in rebellion against Him. Whether you are already a Christian, or not, you must confess and repent of anything in your heart and life that separates you from God and His perfect Will for you.

For your life to become appropriately oriented, you must first be at peace with your God. In finding peace with God you become empowered to also be at peace with yourself and to be at peace in this world. God will grant you peace, perfect tranquility, which quenches the turmoil of any situation that confronts you in this life.

We need to lay our baggage down and find rest in His presence. God wants us to acknowledge our sins, confess them to Him and to be genuinely remorseful of them. So great is the magnitude of our sins that it required the precious blood of Jesus Christ in order for us to be redeemed. What a price to pay! But that is the cost of our transgressions (Romans 6:23).

The good news is that since it is already paid by Christ, we can choose not to re-pay it with our own lives. It is like money that has been deposited to our overdraft bank account and just sitting there, waiting for us to make use of it. That wage is already paid with the life of Jesus and has been gifted to us. This gift is eternal life and abundant life, here and now.

Surrender

We naturally inherited the *seed*, or character trait, of the devil which was planted in Adam and Eve the day they sinned. So our tendencies are corrupt and bent towards evil and destruction, even when on our own we try to live life according to the best we know. However, God plants His seed of righteousness - His Spirit in the surrendered, new believer (1 John 3:7-10). This seed gives birth to a new person, empowered to live a holy and abundant life.

God's Spirit is freely extended to us, but can never take root in our hearts unless we allow this. We must first surrender all. The seed of the devil must be completely displaced by the seed of God.

Outside of Christ, spiritually, we are like the typical un-germinated seed. The un-germinated seed looks and behaves lifeless. In fact, scientists have found that activities associated with life, such as respiration, are so minimal in some un-germinated seeds that it is difficult to tell whether or not the seed is still alive. Isn't that similar to the life not fully surrendered to Christ? Fruitless. Like the un-germinated seed, having the potential to bring forth real fruit but not the ability.

The un-germinated seed is usually in a state of dormancy where it needs something external of itself in order for it to be activated and mature to the next stage. This stage of dormancy for the un-germinated seed is also protective. It ensures that the essential plant material inside the seed is kept viable for a limited period of time until the external conditions needed for germination penetrates into the seed. When placed in this right condition, the seed bursts open with new life.

When Adam and Eve sinned, God could have allowed them to instantly die physically. Even though they were spiritually dormant outside of His presence, God spared their physical life, for a season. This gave all of us the opportunity for His Spirit to germinate in us and grow into our spiritual new life. He designed a Plan to ensure that we could pass from that stage of spiritual dormancy to the stage of abundant life through Christ Jesus. This goes for your life too.

Even in our spiritually dormant state, the protective hands of our merciful God still extend towards preserving us from the whiles of the devil; though only as far as we allow this. But we too have limitations to our lifespan. It is so important that we germinate before this time has expired. While some motivational speakers will say, "inside, you possess all that it takes to germinate, blossom and bloom", I choose to say otherwise. In addition to what you possess inside, you desperately need the presence of the Lord. You need to surrender your current being to Him and allow Him to transform this into that person capable of living a fruitful life.

The un-germinated seed must first abandon its entire current state in order to develop and grow. It must surrender that state of dormancy to obtain new life. Only then can it grow, continuously grow to maturity, and then bear fruit. The seed must give up its entire being to be transformed into a fruitful plant. Before long, no remnant of the seed can be located on the plant that has emerged. The plant is like a new creation in its characteristics and function.

Baptism symbolizes this surrender. You too must give up your all - your entire being. All your desires, hopes, dreams, aspirations, sin, insecurities, faults, weaknesses and strengths to God for Him to mold you as He sees fit and use you as He desires.

Your Creator knows you inside out. Every little flaw, every single strength, He is already familiar with and He already has a plan of how to remove or reshape them and use them to their fullest for His glory.

Like the seed, God will plant you where He wants you to be. He will provide you the right conditions for you to grow, bloom and bear fruit. If a single, seemingly lifeless pea can germinate and grow to produce hundreds and thousands of peas, then what can't God accomplish through any human life surrendered to His Will.

Maybe you're feeling like an un-germinated seed. If so, the Lord has already provided the necessary conditions for you to germinate and good soil for you to grow. *You are alive, and viable!* Like the tiny mustard seed that grows to become a large tree (Matthew 13: 31&32), you too have the potential for greatness in Christ. Trust God's goodness.

When we first come to Christ, we lack that deep rich experience with him to firmly water our confidence in him. If you are a new follower of Christ, it's natural to be hesitant at this stage concerning the consequences you may face as a result of surrendering all to Christ; however, doubt should never be permitted to hold you back from God's great Plan for you.

Peter once said to Christ, "We have left all and followed you!" Christ's reply was that, of a fact, no one who has abandoned all for the sake of the kingdom of God will fail to receive, in return, far more in his lifetime and in eternity (Luke 18:28&29). Today, Christ is echoing this very promise to you. There is far greater to be obtained in the life surrendered to Christ.

There is the age-old concept that surrendering our lives to Christ will result in us missing out on the pleasures of this life. For that reason many lives remain un-surrendered. Or even after surrendering, some of us thwart our spiritual growth and ability to bear fruit by choosing to deviate from God's divine Plan. But that concept is so very wrong.

The surrendered person will miss out on some events that cause temporal pleasures but not miss out on pleasure itself. This is never possible when we are in the presence of the God who created pleasure and has eternal pleasures at His right hand (Psalm 16:11). The truth is, when we chose to go against God's Plan for our lives we never really find lasting pleasure, true joy and contentment. Many, who live in pursuit of temporal pleasure, only find misery and destruction for them and even those who share in their path.

When Jonah tried to escape God's ordained plan for His life he, along with those in his presence, faced such great turmoil that he was lead to cry out to the Lord from the belly of a fish (Jonah 1-2). Like Jonah, we may not instantly fathom the dangers of running away from God's Will for our lives until we approach a roadblock. We may not even grasp the blessings of having God's Will over our lives, until after their fulfillment. However, if we allow it, our short-sightedness and distrust can become a deterrent to accepting God's Plan.

Jonah eventually surrendered his will for God's. He prayed a prayer of salvation and the Lord rescued him from the belly of the fish (Jonah 2:1-7). Like Jonah, if you too sincerely pray this prayer, God will save you and reform you and your life. He will replenish your life with His joy and redirect it on the Path of joy and fulfillment. Why not surrender your all to Him?

People will fail you. Circumstances will fail you. Even you will fail you. I say this with absolute surety: *"God will never fail you."*

Acceptance

One day, an acquaintance asked for my family to share a meal with him because he had nothing to eat. That meal was the beginning of a series of heart-to-heart conversations.

With time, he confided in my sister and I about his notorious past. He had found Christ and this changed his life. Yet, he struggled with the reality that God could fully embrace someone like him, with such a wretched past. He tearfully shared that the love my sister and I expressed towards him is comparable to none other he has received in his entire life. Being loved unconditionally was a strange and unreal phenomenon to his life.

"If God could really love me like the two of you do", he remarked, "I would go all the way with Him". But our love for him fell far shorter than the endless, amazing, unfathomable love of his Heavenly Father and Christ who died to save him. Tried as we may, he struggled to appreciate this reality. He was willing to go half the way. He confessed his sins, repented and abandoned his most notorious old ways.

He stood at the brink and looked over. He saw the splendor that God had to offer but never considered himself worthy to receive it. He believed in the power of God to cleanse him, but not the goodness of God to restore him that special life that was designed for him. For that reason, he rejected to explore God's ideal for his life.

Yet, it never did change the reality of how much God really does love him and the provisions He has made for him. What it does change is the opportunity he allowed God to freely express this unconditional love in his personal life. It smothered the opportunity for God to completely rescue him and empower him to live life to its fullest in accordance with His Will.

God loves you - just as you are. As a result of this great love, He desires and demands more for you and your life. His love for you extends beyond what your human mind can grasp. His power and willingness to not only rescue you from sin, but also freely bestow on you the vast treasures of this life, is beyond your comprehension. Why not accept it. Why not explore the heights and depths of the wonders of this glorious life that God has provided, just for you.

Willingness to Faithfully Follow

During a horse race, the horse is coerced into starting the race and persevering swiftly to the end. The horse is equipped with blinkers or blinders around his eyes. These ensure that his vision is focused before him and he's not distracted by anything behind or to the side, such as a roaring crowd. The jockey's whip offers greater re-enforcement for the horse to remain in the race at a competitive speed. The question is: "how many horses would willingly run to the end if such pressure was not inflicted?"

The difference between God's principle and a jockey's is that the jockey will coerce the horse into running, regardless of whether or not the horse desires to be in the race. God does not use force. While the Lord will invite, inspire and encourage us to journey on the Narrow Road, He will never compel us.

The Lord wants us to follow Him willingly from our own conscious decision. He may lovingly chastise us as a means of helping us to remain focus, but not to serve Him against our will. All who journey on the Narrow Road and enter the Kingdom of God will do so freely, willingly and with a cheerful heart. They would have weighed in the balance the things of this world and the things of God and found it far more rewarding to seek after heavenly things.

When the Samaritan woman went to the well to collect water, she was seeking the ordinary things of this life (John 4:1-42). However, Christ had more to offer her than that which this world could ever offer. He had more to offer than she even recognized that she needed. As soon as she grasped the full understanding that the person with whom she was speaking to was Christ and that salvation was being offered to her, she instantly embraced this.

She could not contain the joy and triumph that she experienced. Right then she discovered her serendipity. At that point, she no longer saw the need to draw water from the well. She abandoned her very purpose for going to the well in the first place. She found a greater purpose for living, than even drawing something as essential as water from the well. There was a matter more urgent and important for her to deal with. She left her water-pot and hurriedly shared with those in her community the good news of what has happened to her. Christ had no need to coerce her to do this.

Following Christ, fulfilling God's Will for her life, became her delight. She had found something precious; something marvelous and she could not ignore it or keep it to herself. She found true joy and the avenue of fulfillment in life. This same experience is assuredly ours when we, not merely seek to drink from the ordinary wells of life but, have found and drunk from the Fountain of Life. When we refrain from chasing after the temporal things of this life and instead make God and the Will of God our lifelong pursuit, this too will be our experience.

Christ used the woman's pursuit for water at the well as an allegory to reflect her pursuit for the things that this world offers. In contrast, Christ pointed to himself as the source of living water – something beyond what the well or this world can offer. Now that the woman has found this *Fountain* from which flows living water, she no longer had need for the water from the *well*. This Fountain is ever flowing with fresh water. Unlike the well, this is not stagnant, lifeless water; but water that springs up into eternal life. This is the difference between what Christ offers in comparison to what the things of this world can ever offer. What Christ offers to us has eternal worth and purpose.

This metaphoric well that Christ speaks about might have included the men in this woman's past and present life that she was looking to, to satisfy her needs. They might have taken the place of God in her life. What are your wells? What temporal things of this world could you be using to replace God and His Will for your life? Why live in pursuit of these wells after you have already found the Fountain?

If for even a moment you believe you can ever live a good life outside of Christ, be reminded that there is far better in Christ. *Life at its best is found only in Christ.*

When we willingly accept Christ, the impact is so profound in our hearts and our lives that this transformation will lead us to faithfully follow and openly declare him. Following Christ will become our delight and sharing him with others, a joy.

His Will for You

"So, I've accepted the Call. I'm willing to follow. What's next?" For some Christians this might appear to be the end but in reality, it is only the beginning. It is the beginning of an incredible, amazing Journey with God!

Throughout life we were groomed to work towards what we want out of life. But now, through surrender, you have transitioned from: "What do *I* want…?" to "What does *God* desire for me and from my life?" God now reigns. His purpose, commands and desires have now replaced yours.

We might have been made to believe that we all must automatically embrace only a general prescription where we join a church, visit regularly, participate in its programs, adhere to its precepts - and it is finished. These are most likely included in God's Will for you, but there is more; so much more.

It is all summed up in the answer to this simple question: "What does God envision for your life?" – Every aspect of your life included. This question is worthy of your personal reflection and is worth consulting the Lord about.

God's Will for your life will usually encompass:

1. His general precepts for all humanity (such as the 10 commandments)
2. Your unique life as an individual

Many pious Christians have learnt from the Bible, God's general precepts for humanity, but have never sought clarity on how God desires to mold and use their lives, as unique individuals. They've never truly embarked on a *personal* walk with God. For that reason, such persons fulfill religious rituals but are left feeling purposeless and unfulfilled. This can be very discouraging. They might even resort to filling the gap of emptiness with immoral practices and the same temporal achievements of this world that non-Christians live for.

Naturally, when the gospel appears to be insufficient to satisfy, it is supplemented with the things of this world. But the problem is not with the gospel. The problem is when our religion is not based on a personal relationship with God; when our individual lives have not connected with God; when our religion has not encompassed God's complete design for our personal lives.

That's because we can never fully live in complete accordance with God's general precepts without simultaneously living in accordance with His unique script for our lives. Can you imagine if Moses strived to live above the 10 commandment but never made himself available to be used by God to lead the Israelites to the Promised Land? How could he honestly say that he had no other God besides Jehovah, if he did not allow God to have ultimate control of his life?

In addition to knowing God's general guidelines, you must also seek him concerning what He desires for you, personally. These coupled together is your uniquely tailored reason for living. It is God's Will for your life in its entirety; His Divine Plan for your life or distinct lane for you to travel.

God designed you distinctively for His Will for your life. There's no question as to whether or not His Will can be accomplished through you. You were designed and are being shaped to fulfill this Plan. In filling you with the Holy Spirit, He has already made available to you the means through which you are perfected for His Will to be accomplished through you. He will also use unique and maybe even diverse ways to communicate His Will to you.

God might place a *burden on your heart*, like say child abuse, as a means of diverting you towards a particular mission for your life. Or maybe He might bestow on you *special talents,* like singing or teaching, and by endowing you with these qualities He would already be enlightening you concerning His desire for your life. Maybe He will place a *special affection in your heart*, like a special love for being around children, and therefore divert you through this means towards ministering to these little ones.

He speaks differently to different individuals concerning His Will for their lives. We must therefore seek to walk closely with Him so that we can discern how He is communicating to us and be empowered to obey.

So how do you know if it's really God's Will for you? God's Will for your life can never be contrary to His general precepts laid out in the Scripture. If you have a burden on your heart to pursue a dream that conflicts with Bible principles, after reading the Scripture you won't have any doubt that this venture can never be God's Will for you. Take time to meditate on His Will for you. This goes beyond a mere prescription that you can read about in a book or discern from your mere human understanding.

In fact, some details about God's Will for your personal life, you just might never know until they unfold. This makes it even more significant for you to ensure that you surrender your entire life to God and by faith allow Him to lead you as you Journey - even when you cannot see where the next step will take you.

God's Will for you is unfolded and fulfilled only by intimately journeying with Him. This intimacy is the provision that He has made through which to guide and empower you in your life's Journey.

God is the only source of the Essence of Life's Journey. His presence, character, power and wisdom adorn the grandeur of heaven and fill its inhabitants with eternal, blissful life. These are the very attributes that are often missing in many lives on earth, yet are necessary for us to enjoy the fulfilling life.

These attributes are available to us. They are available to you. You do not possess them on your own but you need them if you are ever going to be a joyful person and fulfill your ordained destiny here on earth. To obtain them, they must flow from God to you. You must establish that life-giving connection with God, through which this is made possible.

Part 2

Intimacy With God

"Taste and see that the LORD is good; blessed is the man who takes refuge in him." Psalms 34:8

GOD IS THE LIFE-GIVER and He possesses all that is required for us to live this life to its fullest. Having the presence of God abiding with us, recreating us, and directing and empowering our lives is experiencing the Essence of Life's Journey.

So far, we have discovered the true Essence of Life's Journey. We have found and surrendered to its Source. This section will focus on drinking from this Fountain of Life.

An intimate connection with God leads us to surrender more and more of self and to receive more and more of Him. Developing and maintaining a deep, personal relationship with God and allowing His Will to be done in our lives is the only means through which we can truly drink from the Fountain of Life and experience the very best of this life. But there are so many barriers that can interfere with this process, so let's identify them and allow the Lord to remove them.

Chapter 3

Advancing in Your Journey

No Other God

ABUNDANT LIVING COMES WITH, not a superficial but, a deep connection, unbroken communion with the Source of life. Since there is only one life Source, we either make a decision to *live abundantly* or *not live abundantly*, depending on our reaction towards God.

Through the level of relationship we seek with God, we will either settle for the tip of the iceberg or the iceberg itself. Through the quality of our relationship with God we choose to either live a mediocre Christian life or to live abundantly. To genuinely commune with God at the highest level made available to us, He must *wholly* have that place in our hearts and lives that was reserved and ordained for Him to occupy. He should be in control.

It's not enough to merely include God in our life or on our agenda. Our life should become engulfed by His and He should define our agenda. It's not enough for God to occupy the number one slot on our idol list either. Prioritizing God in this sense is not sufficient. He must be our all - our only God. He alone must be depended on as the Essence of your being.

A colleague, who was Hindu at the time, excitedly shared with me that he had accepted Christ: he was now both Hindu and Christian at the same time. This astonished me; I couldn't see the 2 religions mingling together since Christianity is based on monotheism. However, he explained that after he had consulted with his gods about a very serious issue in his life, the issue remained unaddressed for a very long time. He then decided to try praying to Jesus and his prayer was answered, instantaneously. From there he recognized the power of Jesus and included him among the gods that he served.

When asked if his loyalty to one does not conflict with his loyalty to the other, he admitted that Christ was his chief God because Christ has been proven to be more powerful than the others. However, he explained that in the future maybe there will be some things that Jesus wouldn't want him to have; but, if any of the other gods wanted him to, then they would grant it. For that reason, he considered it important, at the time, not to abandon the others while accepting Christ.

In addition to polytheism, there was no personal intimate relationship with Christ. His religion went only as far as appeasing the gods and having them grant his requests.

Christians do not usually practice polytheism in this very manner. But idols in the forms of anyone or anything that occupy our affection or even our dependence, which should be diverted only to God, are actually sharing the place that only God should have in our hearts and over our lives.

When God commanded us to have no other God besides Him (Exodus 20:3), He was pointing us to the connection that we need to establish with Him and the place He must occupy in our lives. We cannot serve two masters (Matthew 6:24). Conflict of interest and conflicting principles will automatically arise between the masters at some point or another, hindering our ability to loyally serve both simultaneously, at all times. Our affection and attention will also be divided.

No wonder God commands us to have no other God besides Him. His goal is to save us from boycotting the undiluted richness that He intends to impart to our lives through this unadulterated relationship with Him.

In His wisdom He knew very well that the presence of other gods will negatively affect our relationship with Him and have a domino effect. It would hinder His ability to effectively work in our lives and would result in us detouring from His ideal Path, even occasionally. *Everything we need in this life, therefore hinges on the quality of our relationship with God.*

God should be:

- the only Lord of our lives
- our ultimate source of dependence for sustenance and security

- the sole recipient of our deepest affection and highest devotion
- our greatest treasure

Nothing can be compared to that unadulterated intimacy with our Lord. Nothing compares to allowing Him to be the only Lord of our lives and having His divine Will unfold as designed. Yet, unfortunately, so often we have competing gods present in the place of the only true God.

Lord of Your Life

God is our rightful owner. Through Christ's death He bought us back from the devil. Moreover, in Him we live and move and have our being (Acts 17:28).

A distinct role of God in our lives is lordship. This is a role that self, anything or anyone else besides God should not occupy, either partially or completely. The decisions made over our lives should never be dictated by our own desires, will and reasoning. They should be governed by God through the principles laid out in the Scriptures. We should also be responsive to whatever other means God might choose to communicate His Will to us. These may include:

- prophets, teachers, etc, that He might appoint to minister to us
- the impressions He imprints on our heart and mind through personal inspiration

It therefore means that God should be consulted momentarily to direct your path, each step along the way - not just with the big decisions but the very small ones too. Every aspect of your being should be immersed under His control.

When God is the only Lord of your life, no matter what, suicide is never an option - because you are not in control of whether you live or die or whatever comes your way. God is.

So often, many of us with full-time jobs complain of not being able to find sufficient time to spend with God or sufficient time to serve in other aspects of life as God requires. The excuse for this is being overly occupied by our jobs.

Time management will definitely be a challenge for most of us in today's society because time is a limited resource in our typical busy lives. However, who is really in control of how we spend our time - God, ourselves or a job? When we find ourselves in this dilemma, the fundamental problem is not so much the busy job. The problem is that God is not in control. He's not given the opportunity to appropriately order our lives. He's not placed in the driver's seat where He belongs. Consequently, just about anything or anyone can push their way in and occupy God's vacant slot.

Whether or not we're conscious of this, the first step we can practically take on the Narrow Road of life's Journey is making God Lord of our lives. We must completely surrender whatever that has been occupying His place, and allow Him in. We must be willing to abandon the life that we've planned and allow Him to guide us into the one He has designed for us. When God is Lord of our lives, He is the one who drives us and direct our goals, decisions and actions.

Unless God is placed in the driver's seat of our lives, and displaces everything else that becomes a barrier to His role as the sole driver, then we will always be too occupied for Him and His Will.

Objects such as our jobs, horoscope, anger, malice, pride, appetite, worries and cares should not be permitted to control our lives. People and self should not be the power controlling our lives either. The devil and his principles should not govern our hearts, minds and our lives. Yet, these are often some of the very things in our lives that rob us of experiencing true joy and fulfillment in life.

When your life decisions are governed by the role of these and other factors, it becomes obvious that they've taken God's place of Lordship. God should be the influence behind what you do or don't do. He should be the ultimate power controlling how your life is lived and your time is scheduled.

Our spiritual leaders or church organization can easily slip into the place that only God should occupy. We should never forget that they are merely vehicles that the Lord appoints to empower our lives and bind us closer to Him. We must exercise caution that their ideologies, teachings and role in our lives - good though these may be - do not evolve into that of our Ultimate Guide. If that happens, their influence can easily be transformed from being a blessing to becoming a curse.

If they fall, you should not fall. If they err, you should continue to embrace God's Truth. If they deviate from the principles of God, on this foundation you should remain firm. This can only happen when you establish your own confidence and guidance directly from God, along with their assistance.

When you allow them to replace God in your life then you would have done away with the very Standard by which their teachings, ideologies and life is measured. How would you then know if they err?

Sustenance & Security

Our loving God, in His wisdom has devised practical ways for us to reap unending joy, peace and contentment in our Journey. The more we immerse ourselves into the presence of God, the greater the joy and contentment we experience in this life. One means by which God empowers us to live the abundant life is by setting us free from the worry associated with cares and burdens of this life, that have held us captive.

Among the greatest regrets of growing up is usually trading in the care-free spirit of our childhood and youth and taking on the burdens of life. A normal childhood is basically about performing chores, eating, sleeping and being merry. What a beautiful life! But interestingly, God wants you to enjoy this carefree spirit throughout your adult life. You get to do so responsibly and have your needs met and your life's mission fulfilled.

You don't have to worry about the finances when you have an efficient and competent Provider and Financial Controller. You don't need to worry about your security when your Body Guard is more powerful than your enemy. You don't have to worry about the next few seconds or the next few years when your future is in the hands of the Giver and Sustainer of life Himself. The power of living a worry-free, joyful life is freely bestowed on you when you seek it through God.

After experiencing an attempted break-in, followed by a break-in a few weeks later, my confidence in Christ as my protector was placed on trial. How safe am I? Was I required to take extreme measures to guarantee my safety, or should I rest assured that I'm safe in the presence of my Savior?

"Even though I walk through the valley of the shadow of death, I will fear no evil: for you are with me" (Psalm 23:4), became my prayer.

"Though I journey on a path surrounded by threats of danger, and even death, I am not afraid of evil. Not because no evil is present but rather, because my God is with me." Shouldn't this be our constant prayer?

It is not the serenity or security structures of our physical surrounding that makes us safe. It is who is protecting us that make us safe. The best synthetic security devices can fail. Harm can ensue unexpectedly in a safe environment. But unconditional safety can be found only in Christ.

It is imperative that we recognize that efforts towards implementing man-made security systems as safety measures are not being condemned. They have their place. This is not the issue. The real issue is that our dependence on security from harm should ultimately lie in Christ - not our circumstances, our own efforts or that of others. Unless God permits it, no harm can befall us under His watchful care. On the contrary, anything can ensnare us when we walk away from His presence.

As with your physical safety, the same applies to your spiritual security. It is guaranteed only through your dependence on God; not from anyone else, not from identifying with any particular Christian group or performing a specific ritual.

A distinct trait that baby chicks have in common is that in the presence of danger they seek refuge one place - under the wings of their mother hen. They're confident about their safe haven. Like the baby chick, you too have a natural desire for safety and security. The bottom line is: where do you seek refuge?

Our chief enemy is the devil. No man-made religious institution or any device that man can construct is guaranteed to adequately counteract his attacks. The devil was created with the capacity of an exalted angel in heaven while humans were created lower than the lowest angel (Ezekiel 28:12-15 & Hebrews 2:6&7). Our human strength cannot be compared to the strength of the devil. Only God Himself can shield us from his snare.

We want to feel safe, not just from physical or spiritual harm but the fear of being exposed to the harsher realities of life, like poverty, loneliness and prejudices. For this reason we can easily create security structures in possessions such as our jobs, family, friends, intellect or outward appearance.

Once more, nothing is wrong with any of these possessions, except for their misuse in providing the basis for making us feel secure in our present life and future prospects. When we place our security in these resources and they are deficient in our lives, we automatically become apprehensive. In this state we can never find absolute peace and contentment.

When our dependence is in our financial status and not in God, if we do not have hefty savings or pensions for taking care of expenses during the most vulnerable stages of our adult life, we can become fearful and worried of the future as we age. After losing our jobs, we would lose hope in living a meaningful life if we trusted the job to provide, instead of trusting God. This is the danger of misplaced dependence. They rob us of the unconditional joy that God is bestowing on us.

As a result of our vulnerabilities as humans we all seek security. So it's very easy for the most sincere person to fall into the snare of misplaced dependence. But everything else besides God and His Kingdom can and will fail. Nothing else is a reliable source of security. *Misplaced dependence interferes with our ability to trust God completely, without reservations.* It interferes with our relationship with God and the level of joy and contentment we can ever experience in this life.

God desires for you to feel safe, without anxiety. He desires for you to find this absolute security in Him. This is a role that only God should occupy in your life. He is a shield to all who place their trust in Him (Proverbs 30:5).

Love and Devotion

Shared spousal affection and devotion can result in devastating cross roads, especially when there is conflict between the recipients. A man who loves dearly and clings closely to both his mother and wife was finally brought into the middle of their continuous heated arguments. The two women competed for the man's affection and just couldn't get along together; however, the man found it hard to let go of either. That is, until he was placed on the spot.

"You have to choose", they both commanded. The man was in despair. Both had his deepest, warmest affection and now he realizes he cannot cling as closely as he opted to both simultaneously. He must choose. He must distinguish between the devotion he holds for both of them and who he will become one with.

No wonder the Lord advised that a man should leave his mother and father, and cling to his wife (Genesis 2:24). There is a special kind of deep affection and devotion towards another human being that should be diverted only to loving his wife. It is the only way he can truly become one with her in a marriage union, without interference.

This marriage union also represents the union Christ desires to share with us. We too must abandon all and cling to God in an affectionate way that we cling to no other person or object. He must have our ultimate affection and devotion. We must love God with our entire heart, with our entire soul, with our entire strength and with our entire mind (Deuteronomy 6:5; Mark 12:30 & Luke 10:27). In fact, this is God's most fundamental and greatest command to you.

Treasure

We should love God like we love no other. Yet, love is something that comes naturally. We cannot feign affection, especially with God. We cannot force our hearts to love someone or forcefully give a person priority in our hearts. Love is based on a number of principles, including the value we place on the person we love.

It's very difficult to speak about our affection towards God without speaking about treasuring Him. That's because the things or people who we deem as our treasure are very intertwined with our hearts. Where our treasure is, there our hearts will be also (Matthew 6: 21). When God and the things of God become our treasure, He will automatically have our hearts.

But it goes both ways.

Your affection: is *influenced by* where your treasure *is* placed

Your affection: *influences* where your treasure *will be* placed

How does where your treasure is placed influence your affection towards God?

The answer to this question is very important since your heart will automatically go after your treasure.

If you invest your everything into building a successful company, due to the amount of energy and resources you expended, the company automatically becomes very dear to your heart. By placing all your treasure in that company, you might consequently place your greatest affection there too.

Whatever or whoever you invest your greatest energy and livelihood into will hold your best affection. If you invest your all in the things of this world, then you will automatically develop a greater affection for these than you do for heavenly things. The loss of such investment would appear to be even greater than missing out on the blessings of heaven.

In such a case, we would seek earnestly to secure what we have found in that valued person or object, at almost any cost. Consequently, that treasured person or object will, directly or indirectly, dictate our decisions, our goals and how we live. Look carefully into your own life and see how this applies. Who/what is the most valued treasure in your life? God should be that treasure. When He is, then He will absorb your best affection.

How does your affection influence where your treasure is placed?

Wherever your best affection lies, there you will seek to invest your greatest treasure. Loving parents would invest greatly in their children's welfare. A loving husband will seek to lavish great pleasantries on his beloved wife.

Peter, James and John were fishermen (Luke 5:1-11). They toiled all night trying to catch fishes with no success. When Christ came on the scene, he miraculously helped the men to catch so great an abundance of fishes that it broke their nets and began to sink their ships. What is strikingly significant is that after this great catch, Christ beckoned to the fishermen to, drop their fishing nets, leave it all behind and follow him. Christ granted them the ultimate of what they were toiling for then gave them the opportunity to choose between this and him.

But they were willing to give up all for Christ; devote their entire life into following him, because this is where their greatest affection was now concentrated. For Peter, James, and John, following Christ now had far greater value than the booming success of their profession. They had a greater love for and have found a greater treasure in the Giver than in the gift. Christ was more worth having. His mission was worth investing their entire lives into.

Whatever or whoever we love the most or seek greatest fulfillment from, there we will divert our greatest resources. Why not ensure that your affection is concentrated on heavenly things and not the things of this earth (Colossians 3:2)? This is exactly where your greatest investment will be.

When God is the centre and theme of your entire life, then every single aspect of your life will evidently revolve around Him. His peaceful, joyful aura will also revolve around you too. When Christ is your heartbeat, every aspect of who you are and how you live will bear testimony of this reality. You will likewise experience the fulfillment that comes only in following after him. You will automatically treasure this relationship and constantly pursue ways of enhancing it.

But, unfortunately, when we value the things of this world more than heavenly things our greatest affections, aspirations and resources are channeled towards the cares of this life. Then, our lives will state that temporal things are more urgent and important to us than our relationship with God.

The level of our relationship with God and consequently our spiritual experience will never exceed the *value* we place on God and spiritual things. What does God mean to you? How does His worth to you compare to the value you place on the temporal things of this life? How much energy and resources are you willing to expend towards fostering His presence and Will over your life?

The parable of the merchant, seeking pearls of great price has such good morals (Matthew 13:45 & 46). The merchant went out seeking. He set out seeking for *fine pearls* so it is quite likely that the ones he already found and had in his possession were very valuable. However, when he found that special pearl of great price, he was willing to trade all the others he had collected for this single pearl.

That's what Christ and heavenly things should mean to us. In our lives, Christ should be valued like that Pearl of great price, outshining everything else that this world could ever offer. And when he does, despite the greatness of our worldly achievements, like Paul we can truly say that the things we once considered as gain, become as filth and loss when compared to the marvelous splendor of knowing Christ intimately (Philippians 3:7&8).

Nothing of this world can be compared in value to the splendor of that intimate connection with Jesus Christ our Lord. But, finding security and sustenance in God, loving Him, being devoted to Him, treasuring Him – making Him our all in all – comes with immersing ourselves into His presence as we journey. It comes with getting to know Him. It comes with walking with Him and finding rest in Christ.

Chapter 4

Abiding in Christ

WE ABIDE IN CHRIST by exploiting opportunities to build our relationship with God. By abiding, we are constantly maintaining an intimate relationship with Him. Our hearts and lives would be constantly renewed, replenished and appropriately directed by God.

The Joy of His Presence

Picture a couple where the loving husband has all that fulfills a wife's needs and wants; and he endeavors to fulfill them. He treasures intimacy with his wife and delights in being in her presence and satisfying all her cares. He loves his wife and goes to the utmost to ensure her happiness and protection. All that he requires from her in return is genuine love and devotion towards him.

On the other hand, the wife values the things her husband offers, but not so much her husband. She will spend time with him, but this time is often dictated by the needs and wants she would like to have him meet. There is no genuine heartfelt desire towards her husband. Her heart is mostly occupied on herself, her needs and desires, along with ways of attaining their fulfillment through her husband. Unfortunately, she missed the point that the best part about being with her husband is not the things that he offered, but in sharing in his presence.

This doesn't sound much like a healthy relationship, does it? Sad to say, it might be the kind that we find ourselves seeking from God.

We should totally depend on God and we must trust Him to fulfill our needs. Our relationship with God; however, should go beyond just having these needs fulfilled. We cannot afford to allow even the gifts that God grant to us, such as our family, our friends, material wealth, and even spiritual gifts to occupy the time and affection that He alone deserves.

Our greatest need in life is the need for God's reigning presence in our lives. We should always be reminded that God is worth having because of who He is and not just because of what He can do for us. We have a greater need for God than the need for the blessings that He offers. Unless we recognize this, we can become so absorbed into going to Him for so many reasons, yet never take the time to go to Him just for the sake of sharing in the joy of His presence.

Yet this is God's ultimate aim in His pursuit after all of us. The God of the Universe desires your company. He's not merely interested in just a formal ritualistic meeting either. He desires for you to know Him intimately. He desires companionship with you. He wants to be your friend, your very best friend. He wants you to share in the pure delight of being His companion and friend.

Christ, referring to us as his bride, demonstrates the heart to heart relationship he wants with his followers. He wants an intimate connection with us in like manner to the relationship that he had with his Father, while he walked this earth. Christ was one with his Father. They had such deep intimacy, that it broke Christ's heart to be separated from God.

The agony that Christ experienced in the Garden of Gethsemane was hardly due to the impending physical pain that he would encounter at the Cross. Rather it was the turmoil associated with the reality of being separated from God. Even while on earth, Christ always walked in the fullness of his Father's presence. They shared constant communion. Bearing the sins of the world had implications of losing this intimacy. It had implications of losing the rich presence of his Father, in order to die for man's sins.

We can consult with the best psychologists, the most renowned psychiatrist, the choicest therapist, yet they can never fully explain or truly quiet the turmoil we experience from a life separated from God. They can teach us to train our minds and adjust our behavior as coping mechanisms for such turmoil. But only God can extinguish the anguish of our souls and replace it with His peaceful gentle Spirit. Oh, what joy, what peace can be found in the presence of God!

There is no substitute to having the Lord continuously present in our hearts, moment by moment - in our thoughts, our motives, our actions, our words and over our entire life. Having Him present everywhere we go and in everything we do.

In God's presence is fullness of joy and at His right hand are eternal pleasures (Psalm 16:11). In God's presence can be found all the essentials of the joyful and fulfilling life. Bask in His presence.

The most amazing aspect of life's Journey is voyaging with God through the presence of His Holy Spirit. He hasn't left us to wander on our own. He promised assuredly that you will seek Him and find Him, when you search for Him with your whole heart (Jeremiah 29:13). He has provided so many means for us to become connected and keep connected to Him.

Sitting at Jesus' Feet

You have surrendered to your Lord and are being influenced by the Holy Spirit of God. However, God does not lead us by hypnotism. He leads us through awakening our conscience, transforming our character and empowering us with wisdom. Therefore, you must first *sit at Jesus' feet* before you can effectively *walk with God*. In so doing, you are brought into the *true rest that comes only in Christ*. Then your Journey would be a life lived under the directives of God - fueled and driven by the Almighty.

Picture Christ walking on this earth in person today, and picture yourself as one of his disciples. Suppose you were to equate the time you spend daily, getting to know God, as time spent literally sitting at Christ's feet as a disciple. Based on your Christian life today, how attentive would you be at literally sitting at Jesus' feet? It is in sitting at Jesus' feet that you get to know God and His directives for your life.

During the time when Christ walked this earth, students would sit at the feet of their master or teacher to learn from him. Even today, we cannot truly serve our Master unless we figuratively sit at his feet and literally learn of him. Today we can sit at Jesus' feet by having him communicate to us: through the Bible, through nature, through his chosen people who speak to us on his behalf, and through songs, prayer and meditation. In our Journey, we can never graduate from God's tutorship.

In Luke 10:38-42 the story of two sisters, Mary and Martha, is related. Though Martha received Jesus into her house she became so occupied with serving him that she didn't find the time to sit at His feet. Not only that, she was greatly perplexed that her sister, Mary, has chosen to sit at the feet of Jesus instead of helping with the serving.

Unfortunately, we too can easily fall prey to Martha's dilemma. We invited Christ into our lives but become distracted by service and never take the time to sit at His feet. It is not hard to see how this dilemma can easily beset us today.

Customarily, as soon as we're introduced to the Christian life, we're outlined the dos and don'ts: the tasks at hand and the ideologies and lifestyle to be patterned as preparation for baptism and automatic reception into that particular recruiting Christian group. For the average Christian, without even realizing it, this recruitment can automatically replace personally going to Christ and finding that new life in Him.

Though such a genuine believer may have never experienced sitting at Jesus' feet, he works piously serving who he knows not. For that reason, he can confuse other folds for the fold of Christ and other service for serving God. He may become caught up in serving self or man's requirements without recognizing it - because he never truly sat at the feet of Christ and learn of Him in order to make this very important distinction.

But for Martha, she was actually serving the true and living Christ. With her, there was no confusion about this. What was inappropriate is that this service has taken the place that the presence of Christ Himself should have occupied.

Serving our Master is noble and it's the delight of every sincere follower of Christ. No wonder Martha confidently voiced her complaint to Christ that Mary is not sharing in the serving and that He should bid her to help. However, Jesus gave a surprising reply:

"… Martha, Martha, you are careful and troubled about many things: But one thing is needful: and Mary has chosen that good part, which shall not be taken away from her" (Luke 10:41&42).

What is that good part? It is sitting at Jesus' feet. It is basking in his presence and learning of him. This is the good part because hidden treasures can be found at Jesus' feet. At his feet, the servant of Christ communes with heaven. Blessings are poured out and the believer becomes empowered to meaningfully and joyfully serve his Master even when the Path becomes lonely and dreary.

Mary chose that good part and she found something special in it. Have you too chosen this good part?

Both Mary and Martha were in the same house. Both were in the company of Christ. Yet, when her sister was murmuring while laboring, Mary found contentment from being with the One in whose presence is fullness of joy. The troubles Martha was experiencing had no residence in Mary's heart because her heart was now occupied with the treasures she found at Jesus' feet.

To sit at the feet of Jesus means to spend quality time with him, moment by moment. It means communing endlessly with God in prayer. This will also include dedicating special time to spend with God in fasting, meditation and in studying the Bible.

What a blessing if you too choose that good part. When you choose to occupy that special place that is reserved for you at Jesus' feet, it shall not, and it cannot be taken away from you because the devil no longer has power over your life. This is the good part of your Journey on the Narrow Road. At Jesus' feet is the best and safest place for you to be.

Praying without Ceasing

Paul admonished us to pray without ceasing (1Thessalonians 5: 17). Likewise, David counsels that those who dwell in the secret place of the Most High will abide under His shadow (Psalm 91:1). Paul didn't advise us to pray on occasions, but to pray non-stop. Neither did David council us to only visit that secret place of communion with God. He admonishes us to reside there.

This council is not to stay on your knees all day every day, without eating, sleeping or going about your regular duties. It's about making a conscious decision to never break that line of communication between you and God. It's about always keeping the line of contact open, anywhere you are and, even when you're not on your knees. It's about not living, even for a moment, outside of God's guiding presence through nurturing impure thoughts, pioneering ungodly decisions and executing sinful deeds.

You must seek to constantly elevate your thoughts to heaven. In everything you do, your mind should be stayed on God and His directives for your life. Be always mindful of the fact that you are on God's assigned Journey and He is the Guide. You need His direction every single step of the way and every single moment of the day. You must never lose contact with Him because the moment you do may just be the very moment that you lose focus and lose your way.

Why not get into the habit of silently speaking to God throughout the day?

When you pray without ceasing you experience heaven on earth. While journeying on earth, you'll experience beams from the magnificence which only angels surrounding God's throne feast on. You'll experience the joy and all the blessings that come with always being in the presence of God. You would be constantly nourished, constantly empowered to live the abundant life and to boldly take that next step of life's Journey.

Prayer and Fasting

To fast means to resolutely abstain from something, usually for a determined period of time. This is typically:

- a complete abstinence from food,
- partial abstinence from specific foods, or
- abstinence from both food and water

Other kinds of fast may include abstinence from activities such as routine work or forms of entertainment.

Spiritual fasting has always been a significant aspect of the lives of God's people. Christ fasted for 40 days after his baptism (Matthew 4:2). Moses also fasted for 40 days when he met with the Lord on Mount Sinai to receive the 10 Commandments (Exodus 34:28). The people of Nineveh fasted in repentance and confession of sin (Jonah 3). When Christ's disciples questioned him about the reason they were unable to cast out an evil spirit from a boy, Christ responded that that kind is removed only through prayer and fasting (Mark 9:16-29).

That's because when prayer and fasting are combined, this is a powerful source of spiritual development and empowerment for God to work through us. It practically enables us to seek God, wholeheartedly, with complete trust and dependence on Him to attend to all of our needs.

The entire existence of the Jews was threatened (Esther 1-9). The decree was passed. The date was set. The day for them to be annihilated by their enemy drew closer and closer. They had practically no escape because they were already in the captivity of those who sought their lives. They needed a spiritual break-through. They needed to hear from God and to be covered under His protective care. They sought the Lord in mourning and complete dependence. They fasted for 3 days. The Lord answered: they were miraculously spared!

Through fasting and prayer we can earnestly approach God concerning any issue on our heart and completely depend on Him for it to be resolved through His Will and Power - not through ours, fate, anyone or anything else. Prayerful fasting brings out the reality that we are not self-sufficient, but dependent on God for our entire existence and sustenance. It brings out the reality that God is our true provider.

Fasting is never to appease God or to be used as a ploy to entice Him to grant our requests. David wrote that he humbled himself in fasting (Psalm 35:13). That is exactly what fasting is. It is a humbling experience.

Prayerful fasting helps us to appreciate who we are and who God is. We are the dependents and He the Provider. As dependent mortals, when we fast and pray, we are actually presenting ourselves before the Almighty God in our nothingness while also depending on Him for absolute sufficiency.

This forcefully affirms to us our great need for God. That's because with the abstinence associated with fasting, comes a reliance on God to fulfill the basic need for whatever we are abstaining from. But this is not all. This process practically re-enforces to us the reality that God is our true Provider and that He is willing and able to supply the need of, not only what we are fasting from but also, all of life's other essentials.

This builds our trust in God and helps us to hand over to Him total sovereignty over our lives. It helps us in surrendering all. It teaches us to wait on God and trust in His ability and willingness to provide for us regardless of what our circumstances appear to be and the hardship we might have to endure. Importantly, it helps us to find security in God and to be assured that all our needs will be attended to, as He sees fit, once we are under His care.

Prayer and Meditation

A function of the circulatory system in your body is transportation of all kinds of substances throughout your body. In other words, the blood circulates around your body as a means of collecting and distributing the nutrients needed by the body and to remove the waste. Both the good and the bad substances that flow into your blood will also flow into the cells of your body, unless removed.

Therefore, your body needs to efficiently eliminate toxins and wastes. This is very important for you to remain healthy and for your blood to be able to efficiently nourish and not poison your entire body. The benefits of the nutrients can never compensate for the harmful effects of the wastes and toxins if left to accumulate. If this happens, your entire health would diminish.

In this manner, your spiritual being is similar to your physical being. Throughout your entire life: morals, principles, stimuli, attitudes and values from your environment have been flooding your senses, mind and thoughts. Some are good, while others are bad. Some are uplifting while others are depreciating. What flows into your being is exactly what will flow into your thoughts, your aspirations, your attitude, your relationships and your entire life - both the good and the bad, if left to accumulate.

Interestingly, the negative things we've been feeding on hinder our relationship with God. They hinder our effectiveness in carrying out God's service. They mar our view of God and our view of His Will for our lives. They mar the quality of life that God intends for us to enjoy by impeding the altitude we will allow Him to take us on our Journey with Him.

When you pray, you simply talk to God. Through meditation, you keenly observe for His feedback to your prayer by giving deep thought to all that pertains to God and His Will for you. You listen to God through meditation. Prayer and meditation combined, unlocks the door to your heart and mind and enables an effective two way communication between you and God.

This provides an amazing opportunity for you to allow God to purge you of all the negative, depressing and demoralizing impressions that have been imprinted into your being. These He will replace with His empowering qualities of wisdom, faith, love, joy and peace.

Great men of God were uplifted through meditation. In the evening, Isaac went into the field to meditate (Genesis 24:63). King David meditated in his heart and explored diligently God's wondrous work, His precepts and His statutes (Psalms 77:6&12; 143:5; 119:15&23). David's wisdom surpassed that of his teachers because he meditated on the Laws of God (Psalm 119:99). He admonishes that we too should be still and meditate on God on our beds (Psalm 4:4).

Joshua encouraged that to prevent God's Word from departing from us we should meditate on it, day and night, to be able to live it; then we are guaranteed of prosperity and success (Joshua 1:8). Those who delight in God's law and meditate on it day and night will be like a tree that is planted by the river; He will produce fruits in his due season; his leaves will not wither and everything he does will prosper (Psalm 1:1-3).

God is constantly communicating to you but it is never easy to recognize His directives amidst the busyness, noise and confusion that surrounds us each day in this world. Therefore, His Voice - His Will, His presence, His principles and His character - becomes clearer and more obvious when you meet with Him in silence and solitude.

Dedicate some special time each day to sit quietly, alone with your Lord. Reflect on the guidelines in His Word. Reflect on Him, His character and His principles. Look around you and reflect on God's creative work. Talk to Him in prayer and listen through meditation. Give deep consideration to His feedback - listen to His *Voice* when all others, including your own, are hushed.

You cannot visibly observe God as you would another human being and most likely He won't communicate to you orally as would another human being. It therefore requires deep reflection for you to truly get to know God and how He desires to direct your life.

Why not arrange some alone time with your Lord today, and even every day?

Like a lover waits gleefully to meet with his beloved, God is waiting to meet with you. There is so much that He longs to empty you of in order to make your life wholesome. So much that He yearns to impart to your life to make it more joyful, rewarding and utterly fulfilling.

It's not enough to just talk to God in prayer and read His Word. Prayerfully meditating on God and His Written Word elevates your thoughts from earth to heaven and unlocks deep insight into godliness and the mystery of His Word. This sets the stage for God to spiritually transform you into His likeness and direct your path in accordance with His Will.

This is because this intimate knowledge of God coupled with the realization of your own sinfulness, presents the amazing opportunity for you to confess your sins, repent and surrender on a deeper level and be able to accept more of God and what He has to offer. Now the gateway would be opened for you to be consciously purified of all that is unlike God and be filled with His righteousness, just as Christ promised (Matthew 5:6).

By beholding the qualities and Will of God through meditation, you will grow to appreciate them and hunger more and more to be endowed with them in your own life. You are elevated to higher altitudes in your experience with God by giving deep consideration to the things of God in order for them to find residence in your heart and consequently your life.

Therefore, why not make it a habit of yours to keep God's Word at the forefront of your mind by memorizing Bible verses. As you go throughout your day you can meditate on a text from the Bible that offers you hope, comfort or advice.

God doesn't just want us to have a relationship with Him that is limited to us going to Him with questions and leaving with answers. For this reason, God may not always respond to us within the instant that we seek to meet with Him and hear from Him in our quiet time. He desires for us to wholly depend on Him and patiently wait on Him. He also desires for us to be constantly communicating with Him.

Therefore, while it's good to meditate during our quiet time, we must also seek to keep our minds on heavenly things throughout our daily routines. So cultivate the attitude of waiting on the Lord and, even during your day-to-day routine, seek to discern His directives.

An intimate connection with God is the greatest experience that mortal beings can ever attain on this earth. The quality of this experience is consequently paralleled by the quality of the life produced. Imagine just how much God can accomplish in your life through simple daily personal communion of deep prayer and meditation on Him, His Word, His Will and His Works.

Studying God's Written Word

There is the old Indian fable of 6 blind men who went to *see* an elephant. One man touched the ear and thought, without a doubt, that the elephant is like a fan. Another touched its tusk and thought the elephant was more like a pipe. The third touched its trunk and said the elephant is like a tree. The forth reached down and touched its leg and concluded that the elephant is like a pillar. The fifth blind man touched the elephant's belly and exclaimed that the elephant is like a wall. The sixth then touched its tail and proclaimed that the elephant is in-deed like a rope.

After touching different parts of the elephant, they derived at different conclusions. With such contradictory and conflicting findings, the men disputed for a great deal of time over their differing opinions of the elephant. They never took the time to return and test the other persons' opinion or re-evaluate their own. Yet, though all of them were to some extent correct, overall, they were all wrong.

Let's say they all went to share their conclusions with their separate group of blind friends who have never explored the elephant for themselves. Wouldn't their friends also derive incomplete and inaccurate conclusions about the elephant?

I have good news and bad news. The bad news is: all who seek to learn the truths of the Bible from their own understanding or the mere human understanding of others will *see* it no clearer than the blind men's view of the elephant. We are only humans, so our understanding can fail us and we may sincerely have misconceptions of truths of the Bible in one aspect or another.

The good news is: our limitation is a reminder for us to place absolute dependence on God in understanding His Written Word. We are reminded to never place our understanding or the understanding of others in the capacity that only God can fill. Solomon, the wisest man that ever lived, encourages us not to depend on our own understanding but to trust the Lord, acknowledge Him and He will direct our path (Proverbs 3:5&6).

A lot of Christians have voiced that they're discouraged from reading the Bible because it's just not easy to understand. The truth is - the Bible is not easily understood from a mere human comprehension.

Understanding the Bible has nothing to do with age, intellect or scholarly achievement. Even religious leaders, prominent theologians and Christian organizations can and do misunderstand and misinterpret significant aspects of the Bible. Some Bible scholars may have a good knowledge of what the Bible says, can rehearse massive portions of Bible text at a time; yet, never fully unravel the precious truths of the Bible.

On face value, the Bible is written in the language of men because it was penned by men. But beneath this surface, spiritually, the Bible is written in a heavenly language because the Spirit of God influenced holy men concerning the content to write. It therefore means that the attempt of ordinary human minds to unravel the mysteries of the Bible will only create confusion and controversies.

The ordinary mind may spend a lifetime trying to explain the Bible as a whole, text by text, but to no avail. The Bible was written by men through the inspiration of the Holy Ghost. Therefore, it can only be perfectly interpreted by men through the inspiration of the Holy Ghost.

If by reading the Bible, we are really seeking for truth; if we're really seeking to have God communicate to us, then we will accomplish this only when our hearts and minds are surrendered to the influence of the Holy Ghost. We must therefore be willing to set aside our own ideologies. While a particular text may have more than one application or morals, its truths cannot contradict from one person's interpretation to another. Truth is absolute. First and foremost, endeavor to explore the truth when reading God's Word.

We must make it our mission to personally understand the Bible, even while we solicit assistance from others. We naturally understand the texts of the Bible through anybody's eyes that interpret - whether it is our own, God's or other's. When we glean from others who read through God's eyes, what we learn is more likely to be consistent with the truth of the Bible. If they do not rely on God's guidance, we will be left with falsehood.

But how can we be certain that the other person reads through God's guidance unless we too search the Scripture under the influence of the Holy Ghost? We are all learners of the Bible. God, the mastermind of the Bible, should therefore become our Ultimate Guide.

Making a decision to interpret the Bible through God's eyes, means being willing to abandon even cherished precepts as the Lord reveals to us that they're not consistent with the truth of His Word. In submitting ourselves under the tutorship of the Holy Ghost, our eyes will gradually become opened to simple Bible truths we might have missed in the past. This has been my personal experience after seeking to read the Bible through God's eyes.

You don't have to be in a hurry to read the Bible in a fixed time. The main goal is not so much to read from Genesis to Revelation in as short a time as possible. It is to know God, His warnings, His principles and His desire for you through His Sacred Writings. So, read the Bible in a timely manner. You may find that you spend days meditating on one particular chapter - but that's exactly how much time it may require for you to grasp to the fullest what God is communicating to you through that particular chapter.

The Bible is like God's letter to you. You don't have to get frustrated when you approach a section that you do not understand. Present it to the Lord and leave it there. In time, He will reveal the interpretation to you.

It was in the middle of King Belshazzar's party that appeared the mysterious fingers of a man's hand writing on the wall (Daniel 5). This strange phenomenon became even more bizarre when the wisest men of Babylon could not interpret what was written. However, God wrote it. And, as complicated as it was, He understood exactly what He wrote. Daniel was a man who allowed Himself to be influenced by God. The mysterious interpretation was therefore revealed to Daniel by God.

The more you seek to read, through the inspiration of the Holy Ghost, the greater will be your understanding of the Bible as a whole and your understanding of God Himself. It is so important for you to set aside quality time to study God's Word. There are so many precious lessons that can be learnt from the written experiences of the Bible characters and from the admonitions God offers through His holy men who wrote (2 Peter 1:21).

The Bible is a collection, of timeless, ageless truth that is applicable to all people and every single facet of life. God doesn't just want you to routinely browse through a few random text or chapters of the Bible. He wants you to search the Bible as for hidden treasure. He wants you to seek for its truth with your whole heart.

The Bible reveals valuable principles to address the varied issues, decisions and challenges you face throughout your Journey. It's not just a story book or an inspirational book. It is your compass. It is the lamp to your feet and the light that brightens your path as you journey throughout life (Psalm 119:105).

Your path is much darker, gloomy, more difficult, and mistake prone when you do not have the correct principles of the Bible guiding your life. It is these principles that God often uses to direct you. Walking around with your meal is not enough to nourish your body. You must eat it before it can impact your health. Walking around with a Bible is not enough to nourish you and to navigate your life. Its principles cannot guide your life unless you know, accept and apply them.

God wants you to understand the Bible to:

- improve your knowledge and appreciation of Him and His Will for your life

- enhance your relationship with Him
- mold your character
- empower your life
- prepare you for what is ahead, and
- share its precious truths with others

Why not make a resolution to allow God to communicate to you even more freely through His Scripture?

Walking with God

So, you have been sitting at Jesus' feet and have been getting acquainted with your Lord and his directives for your life. Now, as you sit with him, you must also walk with him.

In your walk with God, it will become evident that your intimate knowledge of Him and your appreciation of His Will for your life are essential. They help you to trust God wholeheartedly and journey with Him on higher ground until you become one with Him.

To walk with God means to continuously journey with Him in your daily life. It means to abide in Christ. This translates to never leaving God out of any event or aspect of your life, but to live under the influence of the Holy Spirit. It is on this route that God will continuously reform you and your life. You will increasingly experience the Essence of Life's Journey and the richness of the joy and fulfillment that ensue.

It is through establishing a deeply intimate relationship with God that we become an over-comer of all that besets us in this world; however, it is only through abiding in Him, walking daily with Him that we remain an over-comer. This is also your only assurance of continuously experiencing joy and fulfillment throughout your life's Journey.

In any journey, the traveler cannot remain stagnant. He is mobile, advancing towards his destination. The same applies to your life's Journey with God. You should advance closer to Him along the way; closer to becoming the person that He wants you to be and closer towards fulfillment of the goals that He designed for your life.

Your intimate knowledge of God will make the difference in how much you trust Him and how willingly and fearlessly you will consequently journey with Him on higher ground.

Knowledge: Pre-requisite to Trust

Suppose one day a friend came to you with *good news*. This friend informed you that this is the best news you will ever hear. He met a man who offered him the option to hand over to him, all that he possessed in exchange for precious gems. This includes all of your friend's hard earned life possessions, in exchange for assets far more valuable than he could have earned in even innumerable lifetimes. Your friend was reassured by the man that he had nothing to lose, only to gain, from this transaction. All the onlookers further persuaded him to carry out the transaction. Your friend trusted this man and handed over everything to him with the expectation that the promise would be fulfilled.

Now, your friend is telling you about the rewards he has already been reaping and those he expects to reap in the future. He tells you all the wonderful things there is about this man; how trustworthy and reliable he is. Then he eagerly invites you to do the same as he has done.

I'm sure there will always be some kind of doubt about this man in your mind until you have met him and proven him for yourself. Maybe you would want to test him with some of your possessions, the least valuable and the worthless ones, but not all. So, in case he isn't who he claims to be, your loss wouldn't be all that great after all.

No matter how you try to convince yourself otherwise, the very same applies to your relationship with God. To totally surrender *all* to God and walk with Him, you must trust Him wholeheartedly. To completely trust Him, you must personally know Him. You must first develop an intimate relationship with Him.

It's one thing to hear about a person, even from a credible source. But it's another thing to experience that person for yourself. The Bible and nature are invaluable sources of getting to know God. Religious leaders, religious books and other materials can also provide excellent information about God. However, that one-to-one contact that you have with God in your daily life experiences is irreplaceable.

By implementing the Word of God in your daily walk and keeping His promises on the forefront of your mind, you are inviting God to journey with you daily. Being mindful of His continued presence journeying with you, every minute of the day, is priceless. It heightens the intimacy in the Journey.

If you have a spouse, you don't just want to hear about him or her from someone else. You want to intimately know your beloved for yourself. You want to spend as much time as possible together. You want to practically share your life and day to day experiences with that person. You want to share in your beloved's life too.

Trust is an integral part of every relationship - even your relationship with God. But you will never fully trust God if you don't know Him personally and intimately. This is just the way it is. God doesn't want you to rely entirely on another person's experience with Him. He wants you to experience Him personally. He wants you to prove His love, power and faithfulness through your own life experiences with Him. He desires for you to see His character in His Word and experience His re-creative, transforming touch so that you too can reflect His character.

What a delight when you make God your travelling companion. Through that relationship with Him, you will know Him intimately and learn to trust Him more and more. The greater your trust, the more willingly you will completely abandon your own way for His. As you let go of those baggage, you will now be led to advancing altitudes in your relationship with God, as you journey together.

Knowledge: Pre-requisite to Journeying on Higher Ground

The meanings we attach to everything in life, even spiritual things, are often limited to what we know. For this reason, through diverse ways, God seeks to improve not only our knowledge of Him, but also our knowledge of His Will for our lives. With improved understanding, we can become empowered with a greater desire and willingness to walk on higher ground with our Lord – a desire to have that higher, richer experience with Him in our Christian Journey.

Through voluntary efforts, a standpipe was constructed in a deprived village in Africa. Prior to this, the villagers had to walk for many miles to collect water from a well. Though they still had to walk a great distance from their homes to the newly constructed standpipe, it was the best thing that they had ever experienced. The villagers reported that for them it was the best thing on earth. So, they had a huge festival with singing and dancing to celebrate this grand event.

This was a single shared community standpipe - not standpipes in their backyards or facets in their homes. But for them, this was the most glorious event on earth. Why? It's much better than what they had ever experienced before and rightfully, they were grateful. It was also the best they had available to them. Interestingly, it was also the best they know to exist. Therefore, the experience meant everything to them and their lives.

But what if those of us, from more developed areas, who are exposed to having tap water conveniently located in our homes, had to travel to a community standpipe to collect water? Would this standpipe mean the same to us as it does to those villagers?

Chances are, if those villagers knew the reality of having tap water in the home and if this reality could also be easily made available to them, the standpipe experience would have meant something different to them. Though tremendously grateful and overjoyed for the standpipe, it might have felt somewhat deficient. Deep down, they might have yearned for and even seek after more.

Does this relate in any way to your walk with God? As followers of Christ we can easily become comfortable with a low level of spiritual experience just because it appears to be better than what we had before we met Christ. Or maybe it's better than what we see when we look around. This Laodicean experience can be very cancerous to our Journey (Revelation 3:14-19). If allowed to thrive, it can stifle and eventually kill our spiritual life.

It's good to be grateful for where you are in your experience with God. You must celebrate this, every step of the way. You must be thankful for even the baby steps that bring you closer to Him and improve your knowledge of Him and His Will for your life. However, in the spirit of not being contented with mediocrity, why not also explore the richness and fullness of God and what He has in store for you? *We cannot experience the inexhaustible joy of the Lord and the fullness of the life that He offers while being spiritually ignorant or complacent.*

Eternal life flows to us through an intimate, unadulterated relationship with God and His Son Jesus Christ. It comes through knowing them deeply (John 17:3). It does not come through having casual contact with God through occasional prayer sessions or in fulfilling religious rituals for the mere purpose of doing so.

God does not envision a causal or superficial relationship with you because that way you can never be filled with His life-giving Spirit; you can never truly be His child. He wants you to know Him intimately because only through such a relationship can His Will and Life become yours.

Naturally, we live in accordance with our *concept of righteousness* and our *concept of God's ideal for us.* That's because, we will never really believe or even strive for what we do not know to exist. Understanding the principles of God and His Will is therefore critical to attaining that higher experience. No wonder we must sit at Jesus' feet before we can effectively walk with Him.

Such intimate knowledge prevents us from limiting the manifestation of the presence and power of God in our lives through ignorance. It is through this higher experience that we enter into the joy of the Lord and the fulfillment that comes from living under His guidance.

God will not force Himself and His Will onto us. His blessings and endowments are usually in accordance with the measure of our faith and the extent that we allow Him to bestow these on our lives. He allows us to consciously choose to walk into the fullness of all that He has to offer. For us to exercise this power of choice, we must know our options.

God is calling you to a higher experience. He is calling you to trust Him wholeheartedly and to walk with Him in oneness, in His holy presence of absolute joy and fulfillment. Higher than your human mind can adequately fathom is the height of the spiritual stature that God intends for you to attain. This is God's desire for you.

God desires that fallen human beings attain a spiritual stature where we once again connect with heaven. He wants to empower you to that measure where you are completely united with Him. It is not God's desire for you to settle for less than what He envisions for you.

How many parents would be contented if after making the ultimate sacrifice for their child's welfare, the child rejects it and lives at a far lower standard than what they provided for? How many of us would settle for a community standpipe when the installation of tap water in the home is available and readily accessible, free of charge? But that is exactly what we do when we settle for less than the provision that God has made for us to live in accordance with His expectations and requirements.

It is so important that you recognize that God is offering you something greater, exceedingly greater, than what you now possess. This is necessary before you can attain it. You must first feel the pangs of hunger and thirst for spiritual things before you can truly appreciate the need to be completely filled and the importance of making that effort towards fulfillment. Christ pronounced that those who hunger and thirst for righteousness are blessed because they are the ones who will be filled (Matthew 5:6).

If in your heart you sincerely yearn for a higher experience with God, then be happy. As Christ promised, it shall be yours. Seek after it with your whole heart and being. When you do so, God will fill you beyond measure. He will lift you to altitudes you never dreamed of. He will lift you to that elevation where you become one with Him. This should be the goal of every follower of Christ.

Oneness

In every relationship and, more so, in every marriage, when there is conflicting sets of principles, ideologies and goals there will remain a wall of barrier between the two parties. They can't meet eye to eye with each other. They cannot experience *oneness* while being separated by this wall. It is a plain fact.

In many ways our own principles, ideologies and goals conflict with God's. They become a barrier when we choose to hold on to them, while attempting to embark on an intimate Journey with Him. God and everything about Him is perfect and true. Where there is conflict, we are at fault.

As you grow closer to God, as your knowledge of Him improves, He will open your eyes even more to the barriers between you and Him. Starting out the Journey you might never have perceived these as barriers; but the Lord winks at our ignorance (Acts 17:30). He's patient with your short-sightedness and excited to have you mature to the level where He can better expose you to His Will and its deterrents. He's equally eager for you to allow Him to break down these barriers as He reveals them to you.

Just like a father would guide his child and in a timely manner educate him about the small things, then more complex things when he comes of the understanding, so is God's attitude towards you. As you journey together with God, you mature spiritually in your understanding and relationship with Him. You mature in your level of trust. As you trust Him more and more, a complete surrender becomes likewise more practical.

For you to become one with Him, it is only fitting that you abandon your way for His as He continues to open your eyes. Only then can you grow higher in your spiritual experience and closer in your relationship with Him.

Surrender is not a one-time event; it is daily, even momentarily. For you to completely walk together, hand in hand, the walls between you and God must be completely surrendered, thoroughly destroyed, brick by brick.

Enoch allowed these walls between him and God to be destroyed. As a result, he walked with God and God was pleased (Genesis 5:24 & Hebrews 11:5&6). So close was the intimacy between him and God, that no distance between heaven and earth, righteousness and sin, could any longer separate them.

Enoch became one with God. He was never allowed to face death. He passed from this life to live with God forever more. So close was their relationship that God took him in His bosom, where he belongs. That's the level of intimacy that God desires to enjoy with you.

Enoch was born sinful, just like you. He committed sin, just like you. He started out with walls that separated him from God, just like you. You can get pass these walls, just like him. Through faith and surrender these walls were removed from between Enoch and God. Enoch's life demonstrates that it is possible for sinful humans to be repositioned to attain this height of intimacy with God. This is God's delight. This is God's ideal for you.

By allowing God to shed the barriers between them, Enoch claimed the fullness of the Essence of Life's Journey. There was nothing between Him and the Source. Let's allow God to completely shed the barriers between Him and us. In so doing, we will find absolute rest in Christ.

When our life becomes absorbed in God and His Will, our desire for our own will and our own way is conquered. Our soul will now find rest in Christ. We too must seek to walk with God as intimately, boldly and selflessly as Enoch walked with Him. What better way to experience the fullness of the splendors of this life than this. What better way to please God than this!

Resting in Christ

Half-Way-Tree is the name of a major town in Jamaica. "What a weird name?" I thought, until I queried the meaning behind the name. The name originated more than a century ago before Half-Way-Tree became an urban centre. During that era, the location became significant as a result of a huge cotton tree and the purpose that the tree served.

The tree was located approximately half the way of the typical traveler's journey to and from Kingston. Travelers would pause at this tree, from their long wearisome journey, to be refreshed, meet and greet with each other, then continue towards their destination. This became a routine and kind of a ritual among the travelers. The tree and the rest that it facilitated the weary travelers conveyed notable significance to their journey; hence the location got its name.

You too are a pilgrim in this world. If you have been walking with God through your daily experiences, you would realize that the day-to-day activities and conflicts of this life can become wearisome. In life's Journey, you too need to pause periodically, from your temporal day-to-day routine, to be refreshed. God designed us this way. He also designed a plan to make this a reality for us.

The issue of the Sabbath Day rest is a controversial one among Christians. This is not a forum to address the controversies. Neither will I attempt to dictate to you to choose either for or against its observance. However, wouldn't it be good for us to explore how the Sabbath was possibly designed to enhance our life's Journey and also our relationship with God – even if the issue is controversial?

I find it almost impossible to address the Essence of Life's Journey without mentioning completely resting in Christ and making reference to the Sabbath rest (Hebrews 4). In walking in oneness with God on the Narrow Road, we find rest for our weary souls (Jeremiah 6:16) – complete rest from sin and our burdens and cares. The Sabbath also exemplifies this rest. Through the Sabbath we rest periodically, from all the temporal labor and pursuits of this life. In total, the Sabbath renders refreshing for our entire being: our spirit, body and our soul.

The Sabbath is one means that was designed, from the very beginning, for *uninterrupted*, rejuvenating spiritual life to flow from God to the believer, throughout life's Journey. Personally, it is a significant means through which my thirsting soul has been continually watered by the blessings of the Lord as I journey on the Narrow Road. It's like my oasis, my Half-Way-Tree. Through it, I am periodically refreshed in a significant way by Christ, the Living Water.

Let's return to where this all began.

The Origin of the Sabbath

During creation, everything of its kind was created only once and was allowed to either reproduce or be controlled by some kind of cycle. This also applies to the days. God created the first day by separating light from darkness (Genesis 1:1-5). The evening and morning was established as the 24hour cycle governing each day. After day 1, the days took an automatic, cyclical pattern. That means God didn't directly create any day after the first. Rather, He established the subsequent days of the week up until day 7. Therefore, God did no creative work at all on the 7th day. He merely ordained it as the last day of the week.

One might wonder, instead of instituting a 7th day merely for the purpose of resting, couldn't God have rested on the 1st day of the following week, foreseeing that Christ would've been resurrected on the 1st day? Would it have made any significant difference today if a 7th day was not instituted?

The 1st day of the week, and all the days up until day 6, already involved routine work. God specifically wanted another day, a special day of the week for a specific purpose that excludes routine work. This purpose existed before the Laws were given to the Jews. It existed even before man sinned. It existed on earth from the moment the very day itself was established. This purpose is the reason for the 7th day to be in existence, even now. It therefore means we cannot separate the purpose of the Sabbath from the 7th day. The Sabbath would be the 7th day and the 7th day would be the Sabbath.

Following the first 6 days of creation, God did something on the 7th day that He did to none of the others. He *blessed* and *sanctified* it and instituted that day by resting from all the work that He had performed during the other 6 days (Genesis 2:2&3).

God in His wisdom saw the need for a 7th day for a sacred purpose that is not limited to time or season. For that reason, from the very first week, He instituted a 7th day that would last throughout earth's history. He blessed and sanctified the *7th day* itself, knowing it would have remained in existence forever.

The Intimacy in the Sabbath Experience

That first 7th Day, God communed, undisturbed, with His creatures. They became acquainted and reflected on His work of creation. That day was a reminder to Adam and Eve of the identity of the Creator of heaven and earth and the identity of their Maker (Exodus 20:11). That day was therefore instituted so that mankind would never lose sight of the beginning of earth's history, our own origin and our Creator.

In a similar way as Memorial Day or Remembrance Day is meant to keep in remembrance the lives of soldiers who served in war, the Sabbath's *eternal* significance is to remind us of the Creator of this universe, through special commemoration.

If everyone genuinely kept the Sabbath from the first week of creation until now, atheism and the theory of evolution might not have even crossed men's mind. This is because the creation story, through its reflection on the 7th day of each week, would have been a perpetual reminder to all humanity of the truth about the Creator and the origin of His creation.

The omniscient God of love perceived all this when He instituted the Sabbath and reminded His people over and again that He has *made* this day holy and they are to *keep* it holy. When God makes something holy, He desires for it to remain forever undefiled. We keep the 7th day holy by doing the very same thing that God did when He made it holy - He rested from all His work.

To the children of Israel, the Sabbath became a reminder of (Exodus 20:8-11; 31:12-17; Deuteronomy 5:15 & Isaiah 58:13&14):

- the identity of their Creator
- deliverance from Egyptian bondage
- deliverance from sin
- the God who makes them holy

After the death of Christ, the Sabbath maintained its significance to God's people. Those who have been delivered from sin and made holy are in reality spiritual Jews. For Christians, the Sabbath is that perpetual reminder, special sign between us and our Redeemer that we have been born again – we're resting in Christ from sin. We have been redeemed, not from Egyptian bondage, but from sin. The Sabbath points to our Redeemer.

Having inherited that sinful nature of fallen Adam and Eve, prior to being born again, we were in no position to *keep the Sabbath holy*. We were in no position to refrain from our own work, our own way, our own pleasure and our own words as God desires and to find delight in the Lord (Isaiah 58:13&14). But being redeemed has made God's children holy through Christ Jesus; and therefore, worthy to keep the Sabbath holy. This makes the Sabbath a special, intimate sign between God and His redeemed.

Sabbath-keeping is more than merely attending church or adhering to dos and don'ts on the 7th day. God desires for us to tabernacle with Him in oneness, just like Adam and Eve did that first weekend. He desires for us to find true rest in Him from all the cares and worries of this life.

Anybody can refrain from secular activities on the Sabbath Day but only the redeemed person can enter into the true Sabbath rest. Only the redeemed can refrain from defiling the sanctity of the Day. Only the redeemed, who have been washed, cleansed and made holy, can keep holy the 7th Day which the holy God has made holy. Doesn't the Sabbath experience heighten the significance of an intimate connection with God?

I thank God that, through Christ, we are free from the bondage of the law (Galatians 3:13). But there is the extreme belief that this puts us at liberty to live an unholy life, evidenced by traits such as lying, stealing or probably even profanity of the Sabbath. In reality, through grace we have been empowered to live a righteous life. We have been empowered to automatically live up to the standard epitomized in all the commandments of God; not because we're held in shackles by them but, because we have been transformed (Romans 6). We would have passed from sin to righteousness.

The Sabbath was made for man and not man for the Sabbath and Christ is Lord of the Sabbath (Mark 2:27&28). In allowing Christ to exercise lordship over your life also, he will lead you into the true Sabbath rest. The Sabbath was intended for our benefit and not to burden us.

I have found it to be a delight. Each weekend, I'm excited to enter into another Sabbath rest because it's a sacred day when, as much as possible, I set aside temporal things and focus my thoughts and activities entirely on the eternal. It's always such a beautiful experience. At the end of the day I am spiritually replenished to step into a new week with the Lord and to face both the temporal and spiritual challenges of life's Journey.

The 7th Day Sabbath is:

1. A reminder of the identity of my Maker and the Creator of this universe.

2. That day where, despite the complexities and challenges of life, for 24 hours I can put aside the temporal aspects of life's Journey and enjoy undisturbed communion with my Lord.

Each Sabbath is a celebration, with Christ and my fellow believers, of the new life in Christ.

3. A witness to those who do not know my God, that He is the Creator and also my Redeemer. It points to the fact that I have surrendered to my Savior and that I have been washed, cleansed and made whole by Him.

4. A reminder of the intimacy God shared in the Garden of Eden with that sinless couple, the week the Sabbath was instituted. It also renders me a minute foretaste and continuous reminder of the complete oneness I will share with my God and fellow believers in the new earth, when all things are passed away and made new once more.

What does the Sabbath signify to you? Meditate on this. Despite what you customarily believe, meditate on whether God desires to elevate your experience with Him and your entire life, through the blessings associated with spending this day in accordance with His commands.

The Fruit of this Intimacy

Strive for such deep intimacy with God that both you and God can truly say of each other: "My beloved is mine, and I am his" (Song of Solomon 2:16).

Through sincere, deep communion, God repositions your path to journeying on the Path of joy and fulfillment. Not only that, He empowers you to journey purposefully on this Narrow Road, from start to finish.

The same way eating is delightful but also necessary for the body to carry out its function effectively, so is communion with God. Experiencing intimacy with God is a delightful reward in itself. This communion with God is also the means towards the great accomplishments that God envisions for your life. It is the entrance to the real splendors of life on earth. It is the means through which you are equipped:

*   for character development
*   to serve God and others in the capacity that He ordains
*   to withstand the challenges of life, and
*   to enjoy the bliss of the Christian life

In short, you become empowered to live the abundant life of joy and fulfillment.

If you have been nesting in the presence of your Lord it is now time to grow, bear fruit, stretch your branches towards the beautiful sky and explore its wonders. It is time to embark on a steeper phase of your amazing Journey with God.

Part 3

The Splendor

The path of the just is as the light of dawn that shines brighter and brighter until it becomes perfect daylight (Proverbs 4:18)

SPIRITUAL BLESSINGS FROM GOD are lavished on you only as your life is wrapped up in Him. Deep communion with God nourishes you spiritually and also your entire life. It brightens your path and enlightens you as you journey. Through this enlightenment, God works in you so that you:

- develop the noble character that pleases Him
- live as He desires
- serve as He intends

God is the wellspring of life everlasting. He is the sole Source that provides the essence of all that gives life its true value, purpose and meaning. In Him all that really matters in life, is yours – guaranteed.

A casual or superficial relationship is not sufficient to experience this rejuvenating power of God in your life. When you personally establish that one-to-one, direct, unbroken contact with Him, such a relationship brings joyful, fulfilling, unending, unlimited - abundant life.

So far, we have identified the Essence of Life's Journey. We have found its Source. We have also established that which is necessary on our part in order to be equipped for the Journey of the joyful and fulfilling life.

This section now seeks to explore the great splendors that God envisions for you as you journey. Such splendors will be evidenced in your life by:

- A restored intimate relationship with God

- Transformed spiritual eyes, mind and heart: superior wisdom and purified character; that is becoming a spiritually new person
- Experiencing the joy and fulfillment that comes with having your life surrendered to God and having His Will performed through you
- The hope of that ultimate goal of spending eternity with God and all those who choose to serve and obey Him

Chapter 5

Experiencing True Joy & Fulfillment in God

Man/Woman of Valor

AT THE PASSING OF each day, you are a day closer to being the person you will finally become. At the passing of each moment, you are a moment closer to your final destination; you are one day closer to your final day on earth. With each passing moment; with each lived experience, your character is being shaped, stronger and stronger, in one direction or the other.

Have you ever stopped to consider: Who are you becoming? Where is your life destined towards?

You won't just wake up one day and find yourself to be that perfect person that God desires for you to be. It takes time. It requires our effort, perseverance and focus for us to attain just about anything of great value, from as temporal as a skill to as eternal as our character.

The Bible says Christ grew in the Spirit; increased in wisdom, stature and in favor with God and men (Luke 2:40 &52). That's right! Even for Christ it was not all instantaneous. Christ was always perfect in his character from his birth to his death; however, he matured and increased in wisdom and in the bestowment of God's grace upon him. So will you, as a follower of Christ. Your character will also be perfected as you mature spiritually.

Gideon started out as someone who considered himself to be a weakling yet he matured to becoming among the greatest servants of God (Judges 6:11-16). While Gideon was threshing wheat in a winepress, the Lord appeared to him with the salutation: *"The Lord is with thee, thou mighty man of valor"*.

At that time Gideon considered himself to be nothing more than an ordinary man. He was from a poor family - and it doesn't stop there either. Gideon was the worst off in his family. What made Gideon a man of valor was the fact that *the Lord was with him*. He claimed the Essence of Life's Journey. Consequently, he possessed all that was needed to be a man of valor.

This is where the strength, the success, the prospect for growth and excellence lie in the life of the believer. The difference between you being an ordinary person and becoming a person of valor pivots on whether or not the Lord is with you, empowering you in life's Journey. This testifies to the reality that the presence of God in our lives is indeed the very most fundamental ingredient in effectively powering our life's Journey.

Are you becoming the person that God desires and intends for you to become? Or unconsciously, are you daily forming a character that is contrary to God's Plan for you?

Today is the best day to consciously ensure that your character is being perfected momentarily by God. There is no better time than now. God created you to be a person of valor. Like Gideon, God sees in you that person of valor. This potential can be unleashed when, through daily surrender, you allow God to journey with you and build you; build you up to His Standard for your life. *God's Standard for you is nothing less than a person of valor.* Do you even realize this?!

God desires to empower you on this Journey to the extent that you never drag your feet through life anymore. Instead, you bounce with energy, enthusiasm and rejuvenation. You become filled with genuine hope and aspirations. You live each day with joy from the great things God is molding into your being and your life. You live in anticipation and hope of the even greater things that are yet to be established. All of this, God excitedly envisions for you.

When God conceived you in His mind, He conceived a person of valor living a life of victory. Regardless of who you are, regardless of your circumstances in this life, today, you are no worse than a precursor to that person who God intends for you to become. He didn't cast you aside and move on to create someone else to fill your vacant place. You are not insignificant; you are not useless. You are the useful piece of clay that the

Master Potter has been patiently preserving with the hope of molding you into perfection. He sees value and purpose in you.

But like the lump of clay, unless molded and shaped into a useful vessel by the Potter's Hand the true value, meaning and purpose of your life can never be realized. For this reason, God desires to refine and perfect you.

Ultimately, God wants to redesign:

1. your character

2. the quality and direction of your life

God's greatest desire is to recreate you, redirect and replenish your life. This is the only way you can step into the joyful and fulfilling life. Now, you are only steps away from the stature you were intended to attain and the life you were destined to live. Give God the chance to develop you into that person that He conceived. Give Him the chance to grant you the life that He envisions for you.

Often we have been advised the behaviors and habits we need to pattern and activities to do as an attempt to living our best life. But living our best life doesn't start or end there. Living the joyful and fulfilling life starts with becoming a genuinely better person; even a new person. It doesn't start with merely acting like a better person. *Living the joyful and fulfilling life requires not 'acting', not just 'doing', but 'being'.*

God must first equip you on the inside to live the life that He designed for you to live.

- It is only the renewed person that can truly live the new life.
- It is through becoming a new person that you are led to live a new life.
- God will mold His wisdom and character into your being, making you into this new person.

Consequently, the new, joyful and fulfilling life is a by-product of who you have become in Christ. You must *become it* before you can *live it*.

The New Person in Christ

There is a tale by Hans Christian Andersen entitled *the Emperor's New Clothes*. The focus of this story is an Emperor who values his appearance more than his own true virtues. Two pretentious tailors hoaxed the Emperor into believing that they make very expensive clothing of the finest quality. However, they claimed that this clothing is invisible to people who are unfit for the Emperor's position or people who are – well, just plain stupid. As the tailors pretended day by day to weave the make-believe luxurious garment for the Emperor, the emperor pretended to be able to see the garment: all because he was fearful of being deemed stupid or unfit for his position.

The garment was finally completed! (Or, so claimed the swindlers). The self-proclaimed tailors dressed the Emperor in his new attire. (Or, so they pretended). Off went the Emperor to make a public appearance before the entire nation. An innocent child from the crowd shouted out: "the Emperor is naked!" But he was quickly hushed up and called a "stupid boy" by the nearby pretenders.

Soon, everyone realized that no one was able to see the Emperor's new clothes. To secure their reputation, each person was merely pretending until finally, they discovered – they weren't all stupid - the Emperor was in fact naked.

It's important that the spiritual garment that you allow yourself to be clothed in is actually the Garment of Christ's Righteousness that has been gifted to you by Christ himself. This Garment represents the Christ-like character that God desires for you to attain. It is woven into your being when, in your daily Journey, you allow God to transform you into the pure, spotless person that He intends for you to be.

When the real spiritual transformation has not been experienced, as followers of Christ, we can be tempted into performing enactments of expected behavior and deeds. We can get so caught up into what should be reflected on the outside that we become pre-occupied in keeping up appearances. Even sincere followers of Christ can fall into this trap out of frustration of wanting to experience what has been promised yet not truly evident in our lives.

Christ admonishes his disciples to beware of the leaven of the Pharisees, which is hypocrisy (Luke 12:1). We should be godly in not just our behavior and outward appearance but in *who we are.*

If you sincerely believe that you haven't experienced that re-generating power of Christ from the inside, it makes no sense to keep up appearances for the sake of impressing others. Just like in the case of the Emperor, or even the Pharisees, others will see your nakedness through the pretense. This can become a damaging, hurtful situation.

In the case of the Emperor, no such authentic garment existed. In the case of Christians a genuine does exist. Display of the counterfeit can damage the faith of onlookers, and even the wearer. Doubts will eventually arise as to whether there is really an authentic new life in Christ.

It is so very easy to be deceived about our spiritual experience but it's never too late to be receptive to the Truth as God reveals it to us. Once we have life, it is never too late in our Journey to allow God to elevate us to the mark of His high calling.

If you find that you have not been experiencing a genuine conversion, this means that Christ is indicating to you your unmet need for him. You should humbly respond to God's Call by fully surrendering your life to Him. If you feel that God is calling you even now to accept His Call, or maybe to claim an even higher experience with Him, take some time to accept this invitation.

Through deep reflection, you must examine your own life and your motives. Daily, you must genuinely surrender and patiently allow God to recreate you and enable who you have become inside to flow naturally to the outside. Unless you claim the genuine Garment - the Righteousness of Christ – unfortunately, you will miss out on experiencing that transforming, rejuvenating power of God in your life.

God is real. Christianity is real. Having a spiritual transformation, inside and out, is real. Unless you experience this real transformation, you miss out on the greatest splendor and miracle of life. It therefore means that you must seek for and secure this experience in Christ with all your heart.

Becoming a spiritually transformed individual will lead to a spectacular transformation of your entire life. As you can see, God wants to change you before He can change your life. He has to. And when this happens you live life at its highest level because God has placed you up there. Nobody or nothing can dislodge you. He bestows on you all that it takes to live up there. You now belong up there. You would have been granted a God-given right to live life at its highest altitude.

New Eyes, New Mind, New Heart

Picture a situation where a valuable treasure was washed up on the shore of an island due to a ship-wrecked vessel at sea. A deprived man came along, walking on the beach in search of valuables. He came upon this same piece of treasure. He took it up, examined it, and then threw it back into the sand. "This is just a worthless piece of junk", he thought to himself, "I have no use for that. I only want valuables".

Next came along another deprived man. He too was in search of valuables that might have been hurled onto the beach by the waves. He came across the same piece of article. He took it up, examined it and thought to himself: "This must be the very best thing I have ever seen in my entire life!" In that object he saw a priceless gem; the solution that his heart always longed for.

It was one and the same object. Yet, when 2 different persons examined it they arrived at extremely contrasting conclusions. How so? They saw through different eyes, valued through different minds and loved from different hearts.

Differences in perception and affection among us humans may arise from our individuality, knowledge, culture, beliefs or simply our level of spirituality. The state of our spiritual eyes, mind and heart has a lot to do with our perception of good and bad, right and wrong, valuable and useless. If as humans we can sometimes differ so greatly from each other, how much more we and God?

As humans, we create our own meanings to the things of our world and even heavenly things. The meanings we create are often different from the true meanings that are established by the all-wise God. Our concept of morals and values are naturally inconsistent with that of the perfect wisdom of God. God desires to impart His wisdom into your life. He desires for you to be wise in order for you to discern:

- who He truly is
- who you truly are without His intervention
- who you can become through Him, and
- the true nature of righteousness and sin

Only through His wisdom can you:

1. realize your great need to confess and repent of all your sins

2. completely surrender, and

3. allow God to transform you into becoming more and more like Him

It is also necessary for you to discern from spiritually new eyes, mind and heart in order to appreciate:

- the things of God
- the value of the situations that God allows to confront you, and
- the value of the best of life that God is offering you

Only the new eyes can view things as they are. Only the new mind can perceive the true value of every earthly situation and of heavenly gifts. Only the new heart can hate sin and utterly adore the things of God.

Your spiritual eyes represent your spiritual vision. This refers to wisdom. Your spiritual mind represents the seat of your thoughts, reasoning and decisions. Your spiritual heart is the home of your affection.

The heart and mind are often used interchangeably in the Scripture to represent our thoughts and affection. They represent our character. The state of man's heart/mind is naturally impure, evil and tarnished until, as we surrender ourselves to the working of the Holy Spirit, it is molded and transformed into the likeness of God's character (Jeremiah 17:9, Mark 7:21 & Psalm 51:10).

When we reflect on the splendors of journeying with God, for many of us it is the temporal things of this world that first comes to mind; that is, all the earthly things and situations in our lives that need fixing. The danger of this mindset is that we will misinterpret the purpose of some of the seemingly bad situations in our lives that God is using to impart real blessings to us. Have you ever considered, how many blessings has God sent your way that you have mistakenly cast aside as a curse or a misfortune just because it looks bad on the surface?

Like the first man that came across the treasure on the beach, you too can stare at God's blessings and mope and grope about them. You may never appreciate their value unless God renews your being. Without that renewing, the best of us can unintentionally waste our lives seeking after the things of this life that are sinful and those that have no real value or purpose to our lives, while neglecting God's blessings.

As a child, have you ever played that game where there's a series of pictures and half of each picture is covered? Based on the half that is made visible to you, you use your imagination to choose from among them the half-picture that you believe would be the most beautiful complete picture of them all, when its hidden half is revealed. This game is very tricky. Often, the most beautiful half-picture doesn't turn out to be the most beautiful complete picture after you see the hidden halves and make a final comparison.

This happens a lot in life too. Looking from one angle something might appear glamorous or dreadful. We often decide what's best for us from that visible angle only. Or what's best for a particular aspect or period of life only, but not beyond; because we cannot see beyond. Sometimes our concept of best doesn't even come close to the reality of best either. We just don't see accurately and completely as the omniscient God sees. Neither do we value as God values. We therefore need His Spirit with us, continuously, guiding and enlightening us as we Journey.

As God renews our spiritual vision, regardless of the situation that we face, we will come to realize that He is concerned about our overall welfare. Never-the-less, He values the eternal above the temporal. While He desires for you to have the temporal things of this life that gives you comfort, He values even deeper than that, the things of eternal significance.

This was clearly revealed through the wilderness experience of the Israelites (Deuteronomy 8:16). *God will never sacrifice your eternal welfare for temporal pleasures.* You must therefore be made to appreciate the eternal value of the blessings He pours upon you as you journey, even when they come at the expense of temporal pleasures.

Thankfully, when we are born of the Spirit, we become a new person in Christ Jesus, even with new desires (2 Corinthians 5:17). God is anointing your eyes with spiritual eye salve to enable you to see things just as they are, and not through a spiritually impaired vision. He is renewing your heart and your mind to love godliness and attain the stature of godliness that He requires of you. God wants to recreate you spiritually. He wants to fill you with His virtues.

God wants to make you into that person who can visualize the value of the new life that He envisions for you. He wants you to genuinely love and appreciate this new life. He wants you to come to the realization that this is the very best life for you so that you can joyfully choose it. Through a thorough conversion, He desires to equip you to live this new life, to its fullest.

Your New Identity

"Who am I?" This is a typical question that most of us seek answers for as soon as we approach teenage years and even throughout adulthood. As we look for answers we identify ourselves with things associated with our lives. We often identify ourselves with attributes, such as our strengths and weaknesses, background, ethnicity, physical features, profession and socio-economic status. These; however, are just representations of the setting that we occupy in the stage of life. They do not even relate to the issue of our true identity.

Our identities are engraved deeper beneath the surface of our skin, our environment and even genetics. So, what then define you as an individual?

'Who you are' is determined by 'whose you are'. When you have germinated spiritually, you have been born of the Spirit of God. You now occupy the honorable position of being a Servant of God. But even greater than this, you become a member of the family of God. You become a child of God (1 John 3:1&2; Romans 8:14 & Galatians 3:26).

As the blood that flows through your veins identifies you with your biological parents, the Spirit of God that dwells in you identifies you as the child of your Heavenly Father. (1 Corinthians 6:19)

Outside of Christ, who you are, means nothing. But in Christ, who you have become, means everything. As a child of the Almighty God, you are now royalty. You are not just the child of an earthly king but the child of the King of the universe. You are a son or daughter of the King of all kings and Lord of all lords.

What an honor to be called a son or daughter of the Most High God! But this is who you truly are. This is your true identity in Christ. There is no other identity more exalted among the human race as having an identity in God. There's no greater honor that can be bestowed on you, than this. This is all the assurance that you need in this life.

Finding our identity in Christ makes us realize that every member of the family of God is equal and special. There is no first class or second class children when it comes to God. You are not inferior to anyone and nobody is inferior to you. We are all equally special because what defines us is the impartial Spirit of God that dwells in us.

This is also what sets God's children apart from the rest of the world. This is our true identity. This true identity is the essence of who we are. It is rooted in God. All our confidence, strength and security are therefore established in God. If only we will see this!

When Peter secured his confidence in Christ, he boldly walked on the water, but as soon as he began to doubt his capability to walk on water, he sank (Matthew 14:22-33). There goes the conflict between an identity rooted in self and the identity established in Christ. There goes the great conflict between self-confidence and confidence in Christ.

With self-confidence we value what can be achieved through our limited strength and capability. Self-confidence can equip us to excel in some ordinary and temporal aspects of this life. But self is crucified in the true follower of Christ. As Paul said: "not I but Christ who lives within me" (Galatians 2:20). When we lose ourselves and find ourselves in Christ, there we will find unlimited buoyancy; not only on dry land but, to walk on the troubled waters that we encounter as we journey in life.

These changes that occur in us when we surrender to Christ, transform our entire spiritual being: our desires, aspirations, passion, our outlook on life, the way we see others and the way we relate to them; it changes our identity. We are no longer children of the devil but children of God (1 John 3:9&10).

Our spiritual vision impaired eyes become open to see beyond what we once were blinded to. Our lost, hopeless, purposeless life becomes filled with newness, hope and meaning. It is this newly found *being* that openly bears testimony of the Source of the believer's identity. This Source is the foundation of the believer's confidence.

It is confidence in Christ that equips us to excel in, not only the ordinary but, the extraordinary. Objectives that are beyond natural human attainments will now become attainable. Our confidence is rightly placed when anchored on Christ and strengthened by what he has accomplished and will continue to accomplish through us – and not in our circumstances or abilities.

Our new identity that is established in God is the foundation from which God molds and perfects us as we journey. It is the foundation that God lays for us to mature spiritually, bear real spiritual Fruit and reap the rewards of journeying on the Narrow Road. A pure mango tree cannot bear real golden apples. Without this new identity, we would never truly experience the blessings and virtues that accompany the converted person.

The Proliferation of Joy in You

The *Fruit of the Spirit* epitomizes the character of God (Galatians 5:22&23). Therefore the *Fruit of the Spirit in you* is a result of surrendering and having God's Spirit reign in you and continuously transform your character towards the likeness of God. As you mature in Christ, through faith, this Fruit now becomes part of your qualities.

This Fruit is therefore a product of God's work in you. It comes with being recreated, redirected and replenished by God. It reflects who you have become in Christ. This Fruit demonstrates that God is now sovereign over your life. It therefore means that having the Holy Spirit dwelling in you must precede the Fruit in you. The Fruit is the real evidence of the Holy Spirit's re-creative work in you.

In my high-school chemistry class I was so fascinated by mixing different substances and observing the products of the different reactions. There were always evidences that a chemical change has occurred - once the change has really occurred. Like for example: changes in color and odor; the occurrence of fizzing; a change from one state to another, like from liquid to gas, and so on.

Another observation is that the product that was formed in the end was always influenced by the substances used from the beginning. Also, the greater the quantity of the substances used in the initial stage, the greater the magnitude of the product formed at the end.

Our spiritual growth is somewhat similar. What we put in, influences what we get out. How much we allow in, is just about how much we get out. Therefore, you cannot hold back from completely surrendering and being controlled by the Holy Spirit, while still expecting to be completely renewed.

The more complete your surrender, the greater liberty you would allow for the reigning presence and power of the Holy Spirit to work in you. Consequently, the greater will be the measure of the Fruit of the Spirit in you. Having the Holy Spirit in control of your life does not make you God or a god. It makes you united with God. This is the means through which God transforms you into a new person and grants you a new life.

This transformation happens gradually and not necessarily in an instant. However, as God works on you and you mature as a Christian, the internal change will become increasingly and strikingly evident to you. Your entire spiritual being becomes more radiant by the renewing effect of God's work. Also, this internal change automatically becomes outwardly manifested and evident to others. Be reminded, though, that this manifestation is not the *Root*, but the *Fruit*. A plant must take root, grow then bear fruit. The same applies to you spiritually.

Our main goal should be to indulge in the fullness of God, as He makes Himself available to us - this is the Root on which our entire life should be anchored. At the same time, the Fruit of the Spirit is the evidence of this experience. It is the evidence that the Holy Spirit of God, truly reigns in you. Why so? Because this Fruit symbolizes the qualities of God, which originate only with God – there is no other source.

This Fruit is the love, *joy*, peace, longsuffering, gentleness, goodness, faithfulness, meekness and temperance (Galatians 5:22&23) that becomes part of who you are through the indwelling Holy Spirit of God.

This is exactly the process through which joy is perpetuated in your life. You cannot pull the cart without the horse – you cannot have true joy without God in your life.

The sovereignty of God over our lives – recreating us, powering and driving us - is the recipe for becoming a joyful person and living the joyful life. To be filled with joy means to be completely surrendered to God and to be consequently filled with the Holy Spirit. Your faith must be anchored in God for you to genuinely trust Him to do this.

It is by abiding in Christ; through continued intimacy with God, that you will produce abundance of Fruit. Through this means, the joy of the Lord will remain in you and you will experience it to its fullest. (John 15:1-11&16)

If we go chasing after the things of this world in pursuit of this joy, we will never find it. We might learn to *enjoy the things in life* but never find the *real joy of life*. Joy is a quality of God that flows into our hearts and lives only when God lives in us.

The Joy of the Lord is the only guarantee to lifelong joy. This joy is not a mind technique. It is not the result of a coping mechanism. Neither is it a strategy that we can learn and apply to our lives. It cannot be bought or sold. It cannot be attained through another human being. It cannot be pursued as the goal, but ensues only as a result of your union with God. It cannot be derived from events, achievements or anything external.

It isn't even imparted externally from God to you. It is a quality of God that He molds into you when you are united with Him. This is exactly why a superficial relationship with God can never suffice. Joy permeates your being through surrender and close communion with God.

When God lives in you, He doesn't just impart joy alone to your life. He molds into you all the character traits summed up as the Fruit of the Spirit. He gives you all that you need for a meaningful, purposeful and fulfilling life.

All of God's qualities are unconditional. All the aspects of the Fruit of His Spirit in you are therefore unconditional. As the love of God doesn't waver with circumstances, the same applies with joy.

This further explains why joy is not dependent on external circumstances. The joy of the Lord thrives during difficult and unpleasant situations, just as it does during happy times. All aspects of the Fruit of the Spirit combined, pave the road to the glorious life that God envisions for you to live on this earth.

Some events in life, like having a newborn, can be joyful. But they cannot recreate you into a joyful person and thereby equip you to live the joyful life. Only God can. This is the real difference between the joy of the Lord and joyful happenings:

The 'joy of the Lord' is not just an experience - It's an attribute.

To experience the joy of the Lord, we must first obtain this attribute from God. Only then are we equipped to *be a joyful person* and consequently *live the joyful life*.

In reiterating, the following must precede the Fruit of the Spirit and the joyful, fulfilling life:

1. Intimacy with God: Complete surrender and accepting God and all that He offers

2. Becoming one with God

By abandoning your life for Christ's, oneness is achieved through the indwelling and work of the Holy Spirit in you. This becomes evident by the new life that germinates in you. The gap between you and God, created by sinful barrier, would now be gradually closing. As you are molded towards the spiritual likeness of God, you and God are becoming one in desires, motives and purpose.

Intimacy is synonymous with reciprocity. For mutual intimacy to be possible, you must willingly give of yourself while embracing someone else. Spiritually, you must completely surrender your life to God while accepting the fullness of all that He offers. It is that intimate connection between you and God that truly gives rise to your renewed life.

Your first birth gives rise to a life that has potential but not ability to live the joyful life and to live life to its fullest. Your spiritual re-birth gives rise to the life loaded with both the potential and the ability to live the joyful and fulfilling life. It is your old life that gives rise to the new life. But it is only this recreated life that is powered and driven by the Holy Spirit of God. It is this new life that embodies abundant living.

Living the Joyful, Fulfilling - Abundant Life!

Think about your favorite celebrity - someone who lives really large in the sense of what the world perceives living big to be. Suppose you were to imitate the life of that person? How good a copy could you come up with? Do you have all the means at your disposal to even live that person's life? If your earning is in the middle class or lower, then that person's resources may be far above your own. What they spend monthly you may hardly be able to spend annually. Then there arises the issue of mimicking their unique traits.

Overall, there is absolutely no way we can simply observe someone, how the person lives, his attitude and demeanor and produce a 100% accurate copy through our own lives. Why then would God require that as followers of Christ we should live as Christ lived?

Today, in this sin infested world, God still desires for us to taste of that pure life that He gave to Adam and Eve. Christ's life on earth embodied this purity. Imperfect beings cannot imitate the life of a perfect being. God desires for us to literally experience it. Christ must therefore live this life in us through the presence of the Holy Spirit.

It is the presence of God the Father and Jesus Christ in you, through the indwelling of the Holy Spirit, which makes living the new life possible (John 14:1-18 & 17:5-13; 1 Corinthians 6:19).

Some aspects of the Christian life will remain a mystery to our mortal minds. No human being can adequately explain life itself - that breath inside of us that keeps us going. Who knows what life within a person looks, tastes, smells, sounds or feels like? The finest doctors cannot pinpoint life in a patient. They can only observe for evidences or signs of life; but not life itself. This explains why patients are at times mistakenly pronounced as dead.

The same applies to the spiritual life. You, or anyone else, will never be able to locate that new life in you. It is only the manifestation of the evidences, like the Fruit of the Spirit, which points to the reality of this genuine new life.

If the element of our own life within us is such a mystery, it's quite understandable that we cannot adequately explain the intricacies of the existence of Christ displacing our surrendered spiritual life. Yet being unable to explain the breath of life of our own existence does not render us dead. Likewise, being unable to explain the intricacies of the spiritually new life that is resurrected in us when we die in Christ does not mean that a literal re-birth did not occur.

That's right, a literal re-birth. As real as is our first birth on this earth, so real is our re-birth through Christ. It is not figurative. It is not physical, but spiritual. Unless we have been literally born again while professing to be Christians, we would be wearing nothing but the Emperor's New Clothes. We would be in no position to literally live the abundant life of joy and fulfillment.

When Christ came into this world as a baby, he was conceived of the Holy Ghost through sinful flesh (Matthew 1:18; Luke 1:30-35). Likewise, when we are born again, born of the Holy Spirit, our spiritual being is re-created even in the existing presence of our sinful flesh. Though there remains a struggle between the Spirit and our carnal nature, in actuality, with constant surrender we are enabled to live that life of Christ.

God's desire is for you to more than *behave* Christ-like; He desires for you to *be* like Christ. Christ's life is this abundant life that offers absolute fulfillment. It represents the life that is governed by the indwelling Holy Ghost and is consequently lived in accordance with the Will of God.

You must first be transformed by the renewing of your mind; then you will be able to test and approve what God's Will is—his good, pleasing and perfect Will (Romans 12:2). As you are being renewed, you are being enabled to discern God's Will for your life as you journey. Through obedience to God's Will, we find fulfilment in life.

The new life that we now find in Christ is the abundant life that was promised to us (John 10:10). The old you cannot live abundantly - you must first be renewed. The old you can live a life with abundance of things in it, but never be able to live life abundantly.

Abundant, unlimited life is found only in God. Christ is the Way that has been made for this life to flow from God to you. You must claim it by faith. When you do, all the joy, the fulfillment, everything that is required to effectively fuel your life's Journey becomes yours.

Eyes have not seen, ears have not heard, hearts have not experienced what God has prepared for those who love Him (1 Corinthians 2:9). Your human mind cannot fathom the exceeding great things that God wants to impart to you. It is beyond measure, beyond what even you can imagine. God will perform far more abundantly than you can ask or imagine, *in accordance* with His power working in you (Ephesians 3:20). This is the vastness of what God has in store for you.

God envisions more than the material when it comes to abundant living. When Christ walked this earth, he had meager material possessions. Yet, he lived abundantly. This is a clear indication of God's definition of quality of life. As followers of Christ some of us may also have very little material wealth; however, this is not a reflection of the abundance of our life, because material wealth cannot add or rob away from the true meaning, purpose and value of our lives. This is not the basis for lifelong joy and fulfillment.

Living the fulfilling life comes with living by God's design. It can never be attained through living according to your own way or chasing after the temporal things of this world. It comes with living in accordance with God's Will for you. Most significantly, it comes through the indwelling and control of the Holy Spirit.

Just as abundant living is not about possessing great worldly assets, neither is it about living long in this present life. God's intent is even more exalted than that. He intends to fill you with His presence. He envisions the richness of lasting joy, peace, love, fulfillment and all that gives worth to life. In this great plan, He envisions even eternal life for you.

Chapter 6

God's Requirement for Your New Life

Possibilities Unleashed

BEING EMPOWERED BY GOD to live this new life through Christ will convert seeming impossibilities into possibilities. Ordinary lives are made extraordinary. Like Gideon, outstanding attributes you never before associated with yourself can become your identifying traits.

God sees all the possibilities in you, even before you or anyone else sees them. The omniscient God knows every cell of your body. He knows every aspect of your being. He knows exactly how to mold your traits for excellence. He knows exactly what is required to spark you up and keep you going at the right rhythm.

David was anointed to be king when he was just a little shepherd boy (1 Samuel 16:1-13). Prior to this, Saul was chosen by the people of Israel to be their king because they saw much in Saul to be desired as king. But, when God looked at little David, He saw more. He saw potential in David that could be molded and converted into greatness, through which God would be glorified.

Under God's directive, Samuel called Jesse and his sons to the sacrifice where a king would be chosen from among Jesse's sons. When Samuel, looked at the physical attributes of Jesse's eldest son, he thought assuredly that this one would be king, but God disagreed. One after the other the sons were presented to Samuel; but Samuel declared that none of those were to be king.

Jesse brought out all his sons to the sacrifice and presented them to Samuel - except for little David. It is obvious that not even Jesse expected David to be the son chosen by God. Jesse didn't even bother to take the time to bring David along with his other sons to the sacrifice. Maybe even David, at this time didn't see the potential for him to be the ordained king for God's people. But his Maker knew him and saw this potential. God saw David's heart towards Him and David's faith in Him. That was all the potential that David needed to lead God's people, slay giant, gain victory over nations and over his transgressions - and most importantly, to please God.

Possibilities were unleashed in David's life because he claimed God's Will for him. He claimed God's Will when it was impossible for him to accomplish it; but possible for God to accomplish it through him. This is the point in our lives when we are empowered beyond performing the natural and the ordinary.

God doesn't just want you to do well academically, professionally, financially or otherwise. He wants to empower you to be spiritually victorious over all of life's challenges and episodes. He desires for you to be victorious in every facet of your life. He wants you to journey on higher ground. He wants you to rise to heights unknown to the ordinary person.

As exemplified by outstanding people of God, it is a reality for you to become equipped for this victorious life. Many Bible characters have lived this experience and when unbelievers read about it, they say, "Oh, this cannot be real. This is a fable". Why? Because these men of God have claimed a life that is beyond what is possible for any ordinary person.

When Peter walked on the water, it was beyond the ordinary (Matthew 14:22-31). When Elijah called down fire from heaven to consume his sacrifice, it was beyond the ordinary (1 Kings 18:17-40). When Elisha brought the dead boy back to life, it was also beyond the ordinary (2 Kings 4:17-35).

What empowered these people to live and perform deeds above the ordinary is not something that they were born with. It's not merely a trade that they learned or an art that they cultivated. It's something they attained from God. They were empowered by the supernatural power of God Almighty, who was sovereign over their lives.

The mistake that unbelievers make is in not recognizing that these men of God were no longer ordinary men. They were ordinary men who were transformed by the renewing power of God and were thereby equipped for Him to work through them.

Interestingly, this is part of God's Plan for ordinary people, even you. What is impossible to man, God wants to make possible through your life. He wants to nurture you to that stature where He can unleash His power into your life for His glory.

God's Special Assignment for You

Can you imagine being sent on a mission without knowing what that mission is about or whether or not you are effectively fulfilling that mission?

Your purpose for living can only be truly understood and lived when you have found your new life in Christ. In your new life it is such a great splendor to learn your reason for being on this earth. Since genuine fulfillment in life comes only from exploring and pursuing God's Will for you then knowing His Will for you becomes integral. A significant aspect of God's Will for your life is a Special Assignment that is common to every follower of Christ.

Christ admonishes his disciples to go into the entire world to teach, preach and lead people to Him in the same manner that he has done to them (Matthew 28:18-20). This admonition is extended to everyone who has accepted the Call to follow Christ by journeying on the Narrow Road.

As individuals and as a community of God's people, we have a special role in the salvation of our fellowmen. God desires that we share the good news of salvation to all who we can whether in words, through projects, programs, our lives and any other means through which God is leading us. As with the woman at the well, others must know of the great riches you have found in Christ, so that they too can be delivered. The spreading of the gospel is God's Special Assignment for us. Followers of Christ are like God's agents on this earth.

Servant of God

God has the power to work directly or through His angels in communicating to the hearts and minds of humanity. Yet He has assigned us humans this awesome task to share in the saving of the souls of those we journey with on this earth. Just think about it: you who were once lost is granted the opportunity to help others who are right where you once were. What an honor! What an awesome privilege to be chosen as partners with Christ in such a noble task.

The opportunity to serve God and to be of service to our fellow men on God's behalf is just about one of the greatest honor God has bestowed on human beings. In fact *there is no greater capacity in service as in making yourself available to be a Servant of God*. God will equip you for the tasks that He designed you to fulfill.

Every doctor, lawyer, engineer or astronaut must undergo training before they can even attempt to perform the tasks of these professions. They must attain the recognized professional standard before they are acceptable to serve in the respective capacity. Similarly, every Servant of God must be equipped by God for service for God.

You won't go to law school to learn how to be a doctor. Likewise, to be a Servant of God, you must learn from Him how to serve within His ordained capacity. You must stay in contact with your Master. You must sit at His feet. The Bible is always the very best place to begin our tutorship.

God empowers you to serve through nurturing wisdom, character development and maturity of your overall being. You are equipped with the Holy Spirit. Where your human faculties fail, God will work supernaturally through you to accomplish the task at hand. All that He requires is your willingness to serve at His command.

Willingness to Serve

The prophet Isaiah was caught up in a vision (Isaiah 6:1-8). In this vision He was in the very holy majestic presence of God. Feelings of unworthiness overcame him but he was cleansed and made worthy to stand in the presence of God. There was a task to be done.

"Who shall I send and who will go for us?" asked the Lord.

Isaiah's response was, "here I am. Send me."

Without hesitation, Isaiah was willing to be used by God. He was no different from the other people around at the time - except that he was willing to be sanctified and used for God's purpose. Today, God still has a task to be done. He still has a message to be delivered. The vineyard is large. Frankly, it's occupied by many. There is so much work to do but so few laboring on God's behalf. Even today, God is still asking who will go on *His behalf*. What is your response?

The following must precede our capacity to serve effectively in God's ordained scheme:

1. Responding to the Call

2. Being empowered and repositioned for service through intimacy with God

Your ability to serve is not dependent on your own capability. Rather, it is dependent on God's competence and how much you are willing to allow this to be manifested through your life. You do not have to be hindered by being fearful about the outcome of your serving. God is all-powerful. His power cannot run out on you. The variable here then is the limitations you might place on God to use you.

You can limit the fulfillment of God's mission for you by:

1. refusing to explore God's Will for your life

2. refusing to serve in a particular facet of life, place, time or to particular people

3. refusing to serve all together

4. failing to believe that God can accomplish the task through you

5. failing to make yourself available for God to use you

6. choosing to serve according to your own will instead of God's

"How can God use me?" This is a question that all of us must ask ourselves and even God. Instead, naturally, you might still be a bit doubtful and be tempted to ask: "How can God really use someone like me for such sacred service?"

The reality is that God loves to use people like you. In doing so, His supernatural influence is most evident and He is glorified among unbelievers. As we have seen throughout the Bible, there are many examples of people who were at great disadvantage in performing God's Will, yet God used them to accomplish extraordinary things. They were flawed and lacking in one way or another. But they had one thing in common. Despite their shortcomings and even their timidity, they yielded themselves to be used by God as He chose to.

Moses was not fluent in speech yet was chosen by God to represent Him and His people before Pharaoh of Egypt and to lead God's people to the Promised Land. Esther, a Jew during the time of the Jewish bondage to Media-Persia, was chosen to marry the King of Medes and Persia. She was influential in sparing the life of the Jewish people at a time when women had hardly any influence in society. Peter, James and John were simple, ordinary fishermen, yet they were chosen by Christ to be his disciples and to spread the gospel in the world.

God's mission for your life is not an afterthought. You are designed into God's Plan for your life. Through a life of surrender, you're being molded into executing this Plan. God's Plan, His Will for you, is actually the very life that He designed for you to live. It is the fulfilling life.

Your natural abilities are God's gifts to you. It is important that as you identify them, you use them to glorify Him. At the same time, even more important than being specially endowed with outstanding traits and natural abilities is having your life surrendered to God. God is more interested in your availability to be used by Him than He's interested in your own ability or its lack.

You might consider yourself to be lacking in admirable talents and outstanding traits and so you might automatically consider this to be a weakness that is equivalent to a certificate of rejection from serving on God's behalf; but not so. In reality, this is where your greatest strength in Christ lies (2 Corinthians 12:10). By surrendering your all to God, including your insecurities and weaknesses, in the presence of this nothingness, it is then that you are tremendously empowered. This is the great paradox of the Christian walk.

Take time to constantly surrender your will to God. Take time to explore His unique purpose for your life and to allow Him to reveal this to you. Most importantly be willing to faithfully serve in whatever capacity that God reveals that He has called you to function towards the fulfillment of the spreading of the gospel. His Will for you as an individual is also integrated into that of those who likewise are willing to obey Him.

Your Role in God's Kingdom

Significantly, you do not journey alone; God and His spiritual children across the world journey with you. In fact, just as with the early Christians in the Bible, it is God's desire for you to journey within a local spiritual group where you have direct contact with other followers of Christ on a regular basis. Like you, others have accepted the Call to live in accordance with God's Will. This is where your role as a member of God's family on earth, overlaps with that of the others.

Becoming part of a local church or spiritual group can be a significant means through which God desires to use you. They too will share in your Journey, as you share in theirs. Just like a body has distinct body parts that works jointly with distinct roles, your roles and theirs overlap in support of this mutual goal.

Christ is the spiritual head, the brain (Ephesians 5:23). Each person is like a different body part (1 Corinthians 12:12-31). Let's say you are a hand. The hand cannot respond appropriately and help the body in its overall function unless it receives and responds to the personalized messages from the brain. The hand also requires coordination from the other body parts so that they all support the functions of the body.

You cannot effectively spread the gospel as God intends unless you function within the capacity that He designed for you to function. A hand cannot function as it is designed to, if disconnected from the body. This is where the blessing of fellowshipping with fellow believers comes in.

By understanding God's real purpose for fellowship, this can help us to understand whether we have found true fellowship within a particular Christian group and whether God's Will for us is being met through this fellowship. This understanding might also be a means through which God will guide us towards finding a genuine Christian group.

Fellowship has the following main purposes:

1. Worshiping God in unity

2. Growing together in unity

3. Spreading the gospel in unity

A healthy fellowship presents the opportunity for its members to worship together in spirit and in truth, grow together and spread the gospel together. God's people are the salt of the earth and the light of the world (Matthew 5:13-16). These are collective functions.

No other taste can be confused with salt. It is outstanding when present. Likewise, its absence is noticed. Nevertheless, tiny grains of salt must work together to produce a tremendous impact. Let's consider the impact of a single grain of salt in a meal. How significant is this? God knows very well too that that's the same result you might achieve in your best efforts in spreading the gospel throughout the world if this is not embarked on collaboratively with His people, as He designed.

As with salt, so it is with light. As individuals, we may effectively illuminate our homes and our little corner. This is of outmost importance; but so is the bigger picture.

In a very large stadium, no matter the voltage of the light bulb, some areas of the stadium would never be as properly lit with a single light bulb as when other light bulbs are used in collaboration. Light illuminates and it guides. The devil knows this, so he will use strategies such as lethargy, power struggle, competition, discouragement, antagonism and dissention to weaken the progression of God's Kingdom, while strengthening his.

First, allow God to make you into that grain of salt and that beam of light so that as an individual you can function effectively as He requires. The deeper your connection with your Source and the greater your collaborative efforts with other sincere Christians, the more far reaching will be your impact on this globe. Unity is truly strength. God values togetherness. As a member of His Family on earth, God envisions for you to fulfill your unique role, often in collaboration with others, to advance His Kingdom.

Belongingness

We all want and need to belong somewhere and to someone. It is an innate feeling. However, before we seek to fulfill this need we must first become secure with our identity. We must first discover to whom we belong in order to be accurately led to where we belong. This also applies to our choice of fellowship. We must first find ourselves in Christ and recognize His direction for our lives.

Unless we identify who we truly are; that is, who we are in Christ, we will automatically find ourselves belonging just about anywhere. We all have that potential to adapt to our environments in order to fit. This tendency can easily forfeit God's ideal for our lives. It can rob us from the joy and fulfillment that comes only from the empowering presence and Will of God.

God's children belong to God. What a splendor! You belong to Him and within His special spiritual Family of believers throughout this earth, whose goals and desires are consistent with God's Will. This is to whom and where you should seek fulfillment for your need of belonging. This is the true means through which you are empowered to live life to its fullest. It's the only way you will be empowered to have God's Will unfold in every aspect of your life.

I've always been amazed at how worldly people like secular singers, athletes and actors find greater motivation for accomplishing their temporal goals than do many Christians in accomplishing God's eternal Will for our lives. Careful reflection on this has revealed that when this happens it's because, as Christians, we lack the driving force needed to fulfill God's Will. This driving force comes from God through a life that is anchored in Him.

Naturally, we're often driven by the wrong things. It is our selfish desires and pursuits that often drive us so we have to allow God to change this. We have to allow Him to drive us or motivate us through the vehicles He chooses. When you have found belongingness in God and among His Family, the motivation that He designed for you to receive will automatically channel you towards fulfilling His Will.

Appropriately fulfilling your need of belongingness is therefore an essential ingredient in fulfilling God's Will for your life. You may never listen to another motivational speech, never read another motivational book, yet you acquire all the empowerment that you need to accomplish your divinely ordained life-long goals. This is because you would have found your ordained niche. You would have found your rightful lane in which to journey on this earth.

Even the lower animals have a sense of discerning where they belong and how to allow this to fulfill their aspirations for life. Herrings travel in schools, wolves in packs, seagulls in flocks and bees live in colonies. These are social animals. So are humans. We survive better and fulfill God's ideal for our lives when our need of belonging is met where we rightfully fit.

God knows this too and He is eager for you to find this level of belonging in Him. Have you found your niche? God wants you to find that place in Him that He has specially prepared for you in your Journey. Allow Him to guide you to that niche. Among the bliss of this Journey is the reality that you belong to someone and you belong somewhere.

Regardless of your circumstances in this life – you belong! You belong to not just anyone or anywhere. You belong to the most significant Power in the universe and in the most significant Family in the universe!

God offers all that is required to steer your life towards fulfilling His Will for you. This is being freely offered to you. He hasn't left you to ramble around unmotivated and undirected. He doesn't desire for you to seek just about any external source either. He knows very well that none other but Him can suffice. Why not allow your need of belongingness to be adequately fulfilled in God? Why not make God and His Will the motivating factor in your life's Journey?

Growing in Christ

The principles of God must be practically incorporated into every aspect of your daily life in order for you to flourish. You are nourished to grow from strength to strength by allowing the continued presence of the Lord with you and consequently, in living in accordance with His principles.

Growing spiritually is not just about your growing collection of information about God in your memory bank or your increased mental database of Bible texts. It's not even limited to how well you are able to talk about God and the Bible either. Importantly, when you grow spiritually you grow closer to God in your relationship with Him and you grow to be more like Him in character. Consequently, even your words and outward behavior will increasing speak of the character of God.

As you grow spiritually, you will mature in:

- Your theoretical and experiential knowledge of God
- Who you have become
- The way you live life; including the manner in which you relate to others and allow God to use you
- Your appreciation of the presence of God in your life and the Will of God over your life

In journeying with God each day and every moment of the day, He will constantly refine you. This will happen as you feast on, digest and seek to live out His Word. He will mold you through each experience that you encounter in your daily life and each individual that you interact with.

Character Development

Your character is who you truly are inside. It is your character that defines you, and not your reputation. Reputation is merely people's perceptions of who you are, while your character is not limited to what others think about you.

Your character is not defined by who you perceive yourself to be either. This is because our perception of ourselves is not always accurate and complete.

Your character is the propeller behind your thoughts, motives, words and actions. This is what defines you morally.

Reputation can be consistent with our character but this is not always the case. Look at Christ for example. He was far more elevated in his character than in the public image held of him by many of the Scribes and Pharisees. What about you? How does your reputation co-relate with who you are?

Christ's life provides a perfect example of which of the two is more significant to God. God is interested in advancing your character, not your reputation. In fact, your character development could very well be the most significant aspect of your Journey on this earth, because your entire mission pivots on this. It is by molding your character that you become refined and virtuous. Your character will dictate the extent to which God can use you. It also determines how well you will sincerely reflect God's purity to the on-looking world, through your life.

It is therefore best to seek to develop the person who we are inside and allow this person to influence what is seen by others on the outside. In this case, we should make every effort to avoid becoming absorbed into securing a good reputation.

Through lies and deception, many of us have consciously sacrificed a good character in return for a good reputation. In fact, we can blindly spend a lifetime building a reputation while not even a moment of our life is purposefully dedicated towards building our character. In doing so, our lives would have been wasted. God's Will would have been forfeited.

The Jews in Christ's time largely succumbed to this predicament. Their effort went into forming admirable reputation based on good appearance of godliness. In doing this they neglected to divert their effort into allowing God to develop true virtues in them.

When Christ approached a fig tree in Jerusalem, from a distance it looked lush because it had leaves; as would fig trees when they are bearing fruits (Mark 11:12-14). As Christ came closer he recognized that the tree had no fruits, only leaves.

This displeased Christ because this was a reminder of a very similar case that existed with those Jews. They had an outward appearance of godliness but lacked true virtues. Kind of like the Emperor's New Clothes, isn't it? But what a real turn off it is when we meet someone that seems really nice yet as soon as we grow closer to that person it's as if an angelic mask gradually fades to reveal a beast.

The finer things of life cannot be bought; they're molded into your being and your life. True virtues are far more costly than anything that can be traded with money. These are not just handed down to you by God. They are cultivated when you intentionally allow God to constantly reform your character. They are born and polished through consistent molding in your daily experiences with God. This splendor of your Journey heightens as you mature in Christ.

Climbing the Spiritual Ladder

A plant doesn't bloom as soon as it germinates. It must first grow to maturity. Then it is ready to bloom and bear fruits. Neither do great men of God just bloom and bear Fruit overnight.

If you come to the realization that you have not met up to God's expectations for your new life do not be in despair with the belief that you are beyond the scope of God's re-creative power. Once you have surrendered your life to God, He is patiently working on you. There is so much more that He desires to achieve in you and in your life. In fact, He will - just as long as you are willing to persevere in attaining that higher level of spiritual experience in your Journey with Him.

Spiritual growth is the sign of mobility in your Christian Journey. Your intimate knowledge of God and your relationship with Him should be constantly improving. His Will should be gradually accomplishing in you and through you as you Journey. These are all evident in a progressive Christian life.

You can never become the person that God designed for you to be and live the life that He designed for you to live, while resisting spiritual growth. If we choose to live passively, we will remain spiritually immobile. If we choose to actively make an effort towards spiritual growth then our character and quality of life will gradually improve and prosper.

Growing in Christ is so important because when we first come to him, even out of complete sincerity, there remain un-surrendered and undeveloped aspects in our lives that we're often unaware of. The closer you grow towards Christ, the more he will open your eyes to these things. The more you will also mature in your understanding and Christian stature and be molded into fulfilling God's *ideal* for your life.

There are different levels of spiritual experience. When we entered the Narrow Road, we started out at the lowest level, then progress. God wants to take you to the highest spiritual level possible for humanity. So many barriers can interfere with this. Sometimes even religious belief systems can set boundaries that bar us from that higher spiritual experience. This is why the issue of surrendering *all* cannot be over-emphasized.

Even the things that you consider as good should be yielded to the Lord. This is never easy to do. But be reminded that if they're truly good for you then He will leave them in your life. The greater your willingness to let go, the higher that God will lift you - even to altitudes beyond your comprehension.

Therefore, never limit God to what you now know. His desire for you is beyond even your intellectual capacity. Allow Him to take you to that next level, even the highest level.

It is growing that leads to blooming and bearing Fruit. You started out as an un-germinated seed that germinated into your new life in Christ. In growing, you do not remain at that stage forever. After you've germinated, you must continue to grow, bloom and bear Fruit in increasing abundance. You must experience the fullness of your Heavenly Father's joyful presence and the fulfillment that comes with living by His design. Your experience becomes more and more glorious only as you grow.

In fact, to remain on the Narrow Road you must advance spiritually. Otherwise, you'll become easily distracted and dislocated. It's hardly possible to remain spiritually stagnant and still maintain a viable spiritual life. When we're resistant to spiritual growth, we slowly fall into a spiritual sleep, then a coma, then death.

Salvation is free. Being saved requires nothing on your part more than to believe in Christ: confession and repentance of your sins, surrender and acceptance of what he offers. However, living the life of the saved to its fullest will require your effort in seeking after heavenly things with all your heart and strength. (In chapter 4 we have already discussed how you can do so.) Now, continue to seek upward progression. Seek to grow in your stature. Upward mobility is a key factor in the viability of your spiritual life.

Interdependence

As we grow physically we lose significant virtues along the way. To be a true disciple of Christ, we must allow God to cultivate the required traits in us so that we do not resist the means He has chosen to feed us spiritually.

In molding your character, God will reform you in ways that revives some childlike traits in you. To really enter the Kingdom of God, we must be like little children (Matthew 18:3). Virtues such as dependence; genuineness; innocence; purity; aptitude to learn from others; and enthusiasm towards life, living and learning are childlike traits that God wants to flourish in you.

It is such a joy to be in the presence of children because of these simple qualities that they possess. It warms the heart and charms the affection of not just their playmates but us adults too. Significantly, many of these traits enable then to learn and function effectively in a world they enter knowing absolutely nothing about. The same will apply to us spiritually.

God wants you to be like a little child in your dependence on Him, just as a child is towards a parent. This trait should also be evident in your attitude of interdependence towards your spiritual brothers and sisters.

Moses' Humility

Unless we are genuinely humble at heart, we may never be able to learn from just about anyone offering us good advice and support, unless of course that person is well respected or an authoritative figure. Yet this might often cause us to travel a hard road in our Journey in life.

Moses was chosen by God to fill the exalted post of leading God's people. However, He welcomed support and assistance from others. This is seen in his relationship with Aaron, who was on a similar spiritual level as he was (Exodus 4:1-16; 17:8-12). They had a spiritual relationship that was based on the principle of mutual support.

At the same time, when his father-in law who is a Midianite offered good advice, Moses didn't reject it (Exodus 18:13-27). Moses' father-in-law, Jethro, noticed that Moses spent his days listening to the complaints and disputes of all the Israelites and offered solutions, case by case. To prevent himself from being burnt out, Jethro recommended to Moses that he should consider appointing judges if God permits. Moses didn't consider himself too exalted to listen to the suggestions of someone else, moreover, someone who is not even an Israelite. Jethro's advice was implemented and proved to be effective.

This does not suggest seeking advice from the ungodly. However, we would be surprised to see the people God will use to speak to us at times. He will use anyone who allows himself to be used by Him, even a child or someone spiritually younger.

The Interdependence of Elijah and Elisha

The relationship between the Prophet Elijah and the Prophet Elisha is a model example of the general role that the more spiritually mature should play in the lives of the less spiritually mature, and vice versa, as we journey together (1 Kings 19:16-21; 2 Kings 2:1-15).

Elisha was a humble child of God and this trait translated into him becoming among the most powerful men of God. He followed Elijah as a disciple for many years. When the time approached for Elijah to be taken by the Lord, Elisha was eventually granted a double portion of Elijah's power. Elisha found strength in gleaning from a godly man who was more spiritually mature and empowered than he was.

When you are born again, like a baby, you enter into a new life. There is so much to learn in this new Journey; so much potential for personal spiritual growth and so many prospects to apply the knowledge that God is imparting to you. To help nurture you spiritually, God will often use others who are more advanced in their spiritual growth than you are. While you do not neglect the company of those who need your help and support, you must be mindful of your own need for others.

Iron sharpens iron (Proverbs 27:17). God wants His children to grow together and strengthen each other. When a follower of Christ is either young in the faith or weak in the faith, strength and support from his fellow believers should help to foster his spiritual growth. In like manner, as he matures spiritually, he should offer the same support to his spiritual brothers and sisters who need this strength, and the cycle goes on.

In offering strength, each person is further strengthened. It's somewhat like that magic penny that when you give it away, it returns right back to you. It's not God's intention that any one of us should seek to progress on this Journey while leaving the other behind. It's not His design for us to seek to journey exclusively of the community of other followers of Christ either.

The closer our connection with God and the more we mature, the less will be our reliance on our fellow believers for spiritual support. However, we never become so strong where we no longer need the society of believers. We were designed to be interdependent. God blessed us with each other's presence in journeying jointly in order to: enhance each other's life, glorify Him and fulfill His mission, together along the pathway.

As you grow in Christ, it's important for you to recognize how God can use you in ways where you can appropriately fill the interdependent roles of both Elisha (the less mature) and Elijah (the more mature) in your own Journey. You too need people with respective roles of Elijah and Elisha for your life. Who can you become a source of encouragement and strength to? Look around you. Look also for those who can strengthen you as you grow. Allow God to provide good soil or healthy Christian fellowship for you to grow, while you also facilitate the growth of others.

You might feel that you don't have the sincere fellowship that can adequately foster your spiritual growth. If so, be reminded that God is the Source of all that you need. When you have God, you have all that you need. He has already made provision for all that you need in Him and through Him. If there appears to be a lack in a particular area of your life or at a particular point in time, chances are, by God's Standard you do not really need it at this point. He promises to supply all your needs, one way or another.

Ultimately, allow God to be your spiritual support and He will be. God has a unique recipe for molding you into a vessel of honor. Be hopeful of the great work that He is doing in you regardless of the vehicles He has chosen.

You Can't Start at the Finish Line

When this Journey is all over, God's faithful will experience the enchantment of a new heaven and a new earth (Revelation 21:1). Everything will be made new. Everything will be made perfect. You will be perfect. The ultimate reward of this Journey is experienced at this point. Then, we will experience the fullness of joy when nothing but pure joy permeates the entire universe. We will live eternally with God in a world where all things are perfect. Let us keep our eyes on this prize as we journey to the end.

But until we get there, we must remember that our Journey is like a race. We can't start at the finish line. After starting, we must progress to the end. We must never remain stationary, never progressing towards a victorious end. God wants us to grow, develop and allow His mission to unfold and be fulfilled in our lives.

As you journey with your Lord you will pass through different situations along the way. Like a long journey from one city to another you may pass through exciting, lonely and gloomy places. So too is life's Journey. Yet the unpleasant circumstances should never be allowed to rob you of your joy as you Journey with your Savior. The sum total of the Journey is fulfilling, joyful and rewarding when you allow the Lord to journey with you as your Companion and Guide.

Since your Journey is one lived on an earth that is constantly maturing in sorrows, disasters and confusion, God must … and He will empower you to withstand. If you allow Him, He will also use these difficulties to fuel your Path.

To literally endure a long distance race you must be physically fit. Your muscles must be gradually developed for endurance. Physical exercise is associated with the principle of adaptation which states that: our body improves its efficiency, by adjusting to stress from exercise. Over time, the same exercise will therefore have a less strenuous impact on your body. That's because your body develops a coping mechanism that equips it to endure pressure and is strengthened to withstand even greater stress.

Life is like a long distance race. Trials and difficulties can strengthen you spiritually, emotionally and psychologically. For this reason, God often permits you to go through the fiery trials as a refining process. These difficulties will be the thorns along your way.

To be able to continuously smell the perfume of the roses that decorate your Path, you must be able to get pass these thorns. You must enjoy the roses. In the process, you will have to endure a few pricks from these thorns. But rather than focusing on them, indulge in the sweet fragrance of the roses. Amidst the difficulties, take time to appreciate the beauty of God's great purpose in all that He permits to come your way.

You may at times become disappointed in your progress, mistakes and failures. But remain patient with your spiritual progress. God is patient with you. Always be reminded that God has started a good work in you. He will never give up on you. He will continue to perform the good work He has started in you until the very end (Philippians 1:6). Remain steadfast.

God wants you to be an over-comer through Him. There is a special joy that comes through victory over adversities. This is among the greatest marvels of journeying on the Narrow Road with God. The joy of overcoming your sins, weaknesses, difficulties and obstacles, is nothing less than spectacular.

It gives you reason to celebrate and encouragement to face whatever unseen challenges that lie ahead.

To be an over-comer, you must be vigilant. Be careful not to become distracted by anything along the way. There will be intruders, in the form of circumstances, objects and even people, but God will empower you to withstand and stand tall.

When a tiny particle, such as a parasite, enters the oyster it produces a pearl sac which engulfs this irritant. It then secretes natural substances as protection from the irritant. This results in the development of a beautiful pearl within the oyster. Pearls are precious gems; but they're actually formed as a consequence of a defense mechanism of oysters towards irritants.

As you journey, through the indwelling of the Holy Spirit, let Christ be your Guide. Allow God to be your shield and His Word your sword. You too must have your share of irritants on your Journey; because, it is often through the presence of these intruders in your life that God molds you into a precious gem.

Part 4

Abounding Joy And Fulfillment

"May the God of hope fill you with all joy and peace as you trust in him, so that you may overflow with hope by the power of the Holy Spirit." Romans 15:13

So OFTEN WE HAVE the notion that the joyful and fulfilling life that God offers places us in a bubble that frees us from encountering troubling situations; but, not so. In fact, we must be reminded that our situations in life have absolutely no power or influence over the joy of the Lord and the fulfillment that comes in being obedient to His Will. We should never forget that the life of those who journey with God is like a battlefield – challenges will come our way. Never-the-less God has blessed us with His presence and the spiritual blessings that ensue.

The joy and fulfillment that comes through experiencing the Essence of Life's Journey are God's gift to you. If not careful, though these are bestowed on you through intimacy with God, your difficulties can make them no more delightful than that Christmas present or wedding gift that remained unopened and unused.

But I have good news: there is joy and fulfillment on the mountain top and even down in the valley. This section will focus on anchoring your confidence in God and exploiting the blessings that ensue, even in the midst of your adversities.

Chapter 7

Joy & Fulfillment Down in the Valley

The Silver-lining behind your Dark Clouds

THERE ARE TIMES IN our Journey that we all experience very trying situations. Of themselves, these situations offer no happiness, strength, assurance, hope or consolation for you to pass through victoriously. However the continued presence of your Lord and Savior journeying with you makes all the difference. Christ, and him alone can grant you the peace that is beyond all understanding (Philippians 4:7). When you trust God, this peace is assuredly yours in any situation.

Overcoming difficulties are significant milestones in our spiritual walk. It is in these critical times, more than ever, that the importance of Christ being Lord of our lives, and the reality of our submission to his lordship, becomes most evident. Through our trials, it is revealed whether or not our faith lies in our own strength, the things of this world, comfortable circumstances, or in Christ. Tribulation is the true test of whether or not we are experiencing the sovereignty of God over our entire life.

Additionally, while our character is being tested, through submission to God, it is also being refined and perfected. We are reminded to consider it pure joy when we are confronted with trials of all kinds because the testing of our faith produces perseverance (James 1:2).

When you abide under the shadow of the Almighty God, as you pass through the refining fiery furnace you will realize that though everything around you crumbles, nothing will disturb your peace. Nothing can! God doesn't intend for the joy and fulfillment associated with His reigning presence in your life to be a temporary or seasonal experience. When you are experiencing the Essence of Life's Journey, you'll have joy and peace even in the middle of a depressing crisis. God's presence in you and with you will secure you and reform you into that person who can withstand anything that the Lord allows to come your way.

Therefore, at your mid-night, let your eyes be firmly focused on your Savior instead of being hypnotized by your depressing circumstances. Regardless of whatever befalls you, maintain your dependence on the solid Anchor that can weather any storm. When you place your faith and confidence entirely in God, your faith will never waver with your changing circumstances.

Whether you lose your job, your family, your reputation, your health, your home, your financial status, or any possession of great value to you, you would still have reason to remain hopeful. Though these possess great significance to your life and their loss is equally devastating, you would still possess Someone greater and, difficult though the battle may be, the reality is that He sustains you. He goes even beyond merely sustaining you, to offering all the contentment that you need in this life.

Through the darkest hours, having God journeying with you will often be the single determining factor between despair and hope, depression and joy, internal confusion and peace, suicidal thoughts and the will to live. These trying circumstances confirm that God's presence in you, directing you and empowering your life is truly all that you need. If you allow it, He will use these difficulties to strengthen your relationship with Him and through His presence, displace the cloud of darkness over your Path.

Difficulties will spring up along the Christian's pathway as a:

- Refining process
- Test of our faith in God and our connection to Him
- Medium through which God is glorified
- Consequence of the sin-polluted world that we live in

Always be reminded that no tragedy that befalls you, as a child of God, doesn't have good, even hidden, somewhere in it.

The Challenging Hurdles

For 40 long years, the Israelites journeyed through the dangerous and depressing wilderness towards Canaan, the Promised Land (Deuteronomy

29:5). This journey could have lasted less than one month had not God directed them through a longer route.

The Israelites were actually returning to possess the land that their forefathers occupied before going to Egypt. After 430 years in Egypt, the present generation of Israelites involved in this returning exodus to Canaan had no experience of living outside of Egypt and outside of Egyptian customs. They can only rely on stories. Plus, living among the Egyptians over 4 centuries had diminished their knowledge of God and faith in Him.

To complicate things, a mixed multitude of people left Egypt for Canaan, with the Israelites (Exodus 12:38). This indicates the presence of people who might not have had a personal contact with the God of Israel but only learnt about Him through their acquaintance with the Israelites while in Egypt. The Israelites were aware of the God of Abraham, Isaac and Jacob; however, did they know Him and claim Him as their personal God? This was tested and proven through their protracted journey in the wilderness.

God deliberately did not lead them through the shorter journey that passes through the land of the Philistines, knowing that their lack of faith in Him might have caused them to return to Egypt when confronted with war (Exodus 13:17 & 18). God saw way ahead of their journey and guided them in their best interest. Unfortunately, their myopic vision could not look beyond their situation to see just how much God has saved them from and that His decision was made to compensate for their weaknesses, and not to harm them.

Instead, they murmured along the way, complaining that God brought them through the wilderness to die. Yet the loving Lord faithfully guided them, even when they did not acknowledge His goodness towards them. Because of unfaithfulness, most of them didn't even live to experience the fulfillment of God's Plan for them.

In our own life's Journey, sometimes our own shortcomings can delay and even prevent God's plans for our lives. It's crucial that we accept by faith, whatever lesson that God is trying to impart through our challenges. This is never easy to do. But we must.

God has great plans in store for you. As a result, He may at times direct you through a wilderness journey as a means of purifying you - building you, preparing you - to enter into His great plans for your life.

When God calls us from our old life to the new, or to a higher rung in our renewed life, we must often enter into a refining process to shed our old traits and have them replaced by His true virtues. This was intended to be the experience of the Israelites in the wilderness. God was purifying them to live the new life He designed for them in Canaan, their Promised Land.

Is God doing something similar for your life too? Is He refining you for that promised life? Whenever you're confronted with a challenging hurdle, trust God's hindsight and His goodwill towards you. Find comfort in His promises, joy in His presence and fulfillment through obedience to His Will.

Look for the Evidences of your Invisible God

There might be times when our difficulties feel so paramount that we cannot perceive any good surrounding our situation or the likelihood of it ever improving. In fact we might feel so alone and downcast that we may not even acknowledge or appreciate the loving and compassionate hands of God laboring in our support.

Always be reminded that your Heavenly Father knows you inside out. He understands your insecurities, weaknesses and vulnerabilities even better than you do. Sometimes He will make decisions along the pathway that you will never completely understand. God is conscious of this and desires to comfort and reassure you. Importantly, He requires that you trust Him and seek to discern His presence in your life, regardless of what your situation looks like.

Throughout the journey God never left the Israelites to wander helplessly and alone in the wilderness. He was always there. And knowing their limited faith in Him and knowledge of Him, He provided visible evidence of His presence among them. This was to ensure that despite the circumstances they encounter, they never lose hope that He is present and directing them as they journey.

In the day He directed them by a pillar of cloud and in the night He led them by a pillar of fire, to provide light and direction (Exodus 13:21 &22). What a compassionate, amazing and understanding God! He meets us just where we are. You don't have to worry about being too far below His level. He will pick you up and exalt you to the stature that brings you closer to Him if you present yourself to Him, humbly, like His little child.

So if after surrendering your all to God, there remains a lingering feeling of being distant from Him, be reassured that it's only just a feeling. He is there, right there in you and with you, regardless of your circumstance in life. Be hopeful and look for the evidences of the presence of your invisible God (Hebrews 11:1).

Are you aware of the evidences of God's guidance in your life? What and/ or who are His pillar of cloud and His pillar of fire in your life? Be grateful for these.

Faith and Gratitude

Sometimes the hurdles may seem so difficult to cross over that you may be tempted to feel that God is punishing you or has abandoned you because of some mistake that you've made. What we often do not ponder is, despite the challenges, just how much has God rescued us from in order to save us, have His ultimate Plan fulfilled in our lives and to keep us on the Narrow Road? Where would you have been, had He not intervened?

Regardless of your circumstances trust the goodness of God towards you. Despite the difficulties, He's always with you just as long as you have not abandoned Him along the way. If you have abandoned Him, you may not know how to find your way back, but He knows how to find you. All that He requires is your willingness to trust Him, abandon your all and follow Him.

When David was disheartened by a crisis in his life, his question to himself was: "Why so cast down, oh my soul?" His solution is to go to his God – his Exceeding Joy – with praise and to hope in Him. (Psalm 43)

In everything, let's give God thanks (1 Thessalonians 5:18). You might not be happy for the troubling situation itself that you face; but in any situation, there are still blessings to be grateful for. In fact, there is no greater blessing than having the presence of God in your life.

Let's allow the Lord to teach us to look for His blessings and learn to be grateful for them, even in the most trying times. A heart of gratitude empowers us to endure difficult times, respond in accordance with God's Will and be able to see His hand in our lives despite our challenges. Gratitude is like a key that unchains the joy of the Lord in our lives during difficult times.

As illogical as this might sound, let us learn to be thankful to our loving and all-knowing God for even the challenges that He allows our way. He allows all things for good. We may not see the good as we journey through our trials, but after all, isn't that what genuine faith is about? Believing the invisible; faith is believing in the goodness and fidelity of God towards us even when it's not plainly visible to us (Hebrews 11:1)).

God's good intention in allowing our difficult hurdles in our lives may not be applicable to our personal lives only, but also for the purpose of glorifying Him for the sake of unbelievers or to uplift the faith of others. God desires to reveal His power and sovereignty through the presence of our nothingness, brokenness and despair. The God who formed a perfect man from filthy dust is both willing and able to shape any bad situation into something good. He desires for us to be practically reminded of this reality.

Yet, there are times when God will never intervene miraculously or even improve our trying situation. He may never explicitly bring to our awareness the reasons for our struggle either. Therefore, we may never be able to see or understand any good reason for all the difficulties we encounter. There is satisfaction that comes from seeking closure. But understanding the reasons behind our hurdles isn't half as important as endeavoring to cross over them according to God's Plan. Faith is by far more important than closure.

In trusting God's goodness towards us we learn to appreciate whatever He allows to come our way, while we're under His protective care. In knowing that anything that befalls God's children can never be outside of His Will, offers enough reassurance for us to persevere with confidence, joy and thanksgiving.

When we trust the Lord to bear our burdens for us, the challenges along our Journey are by far more tolerable and worth enduring. When we're carrying a physical load it naturally leaves an impact on us. The Longer we bear the load and the heavier the load, the greater the impact. It's only natural. The same goes for our challenges. The impact of carrying every kind of burden in life is felt.

For instance, the psychology class was just about dismissed when the lecturer pulled out an optical illusion drawing for our analysis. It was just before lunch time. Everyone was feeling the pangs from their empty stomach, so although the diagram really depicted a face, we all saw some form of food.

The same occurs with our outlook on our life while we choose to carry the burden of our difficulties. Our spiritual vision can become impaired and it becomes very hard for us to discern the reality of God's presence, His blessings and His Will for our lives. We easily become discouraged, spiritually disoriented and distracted by our challenges during this state.

Christ invites you to cast your burdens on him because he cares for you (1 Peter 5:7). To cast your burdens on the Lord means trusting Him to manage your difficulties and to work things out for the very best. It means being able to find peace and comfort in Him even in the midst of your trials. When this happens you will find yourself not being worried about the reality of enduring the difficulty or facing an undesirable outcome at the end of it all. In return, this saves you from so much mental and psychological despair.

Instead of being weighed down by your difficulties, why not choose to divert your focus towards enjoying the presence of the Lord, being hopeful, finding comfort in His promises and fulfillment in His Will? Be joyful in hope, patient in your affliction and persistent in prayer (Romans 12:12).

Ditching the Hurdles

Jacob saw a hurdle in his life that obviously had no legitimate way of crossing (Genesis 25:20-34; 27). He was second in birth to His twin brother Esau, but God ordained him to be the rightful heir to the blessings of the birthright. Although unaware to Jacob, God had His own ideal plans of executing this and everything else that He ordains.

Unfortunately, as we know, Jacob took matters in his own hands. He tricked Esau into selling him his birthright for a pot of soup when Esau was faint for food. To make matters worse, Jacob further tricked his father into giving him Esau's blessing. Jacob's swindling attitude angered his brother and created such raging enmity, that Jacob had to flee his country out of fear that Esau would kill him.

What Jacob did not realize was that the birthright that was promised by God was a sure promise. It was already his by faith. God promised it, so it had to be his. Jacob wasted his time and energy outsmarting his father and brother merely because he saw a dilemma that he thought would prevent God's promise from being fulfilled. He saw a discrepancy in being both the second born and heir, while his older brother was still alive. Not only that, by attempting to ditch this hurdle, he multiplied it and suffered the repercussions of his unbelief.

In life's Journey, when confronted with a crisis we're often tempted to pursue the easiest and not necessarily the best route. As humans, our first instinct is naturally to avoid trials and pain, to the extent where we often settle for resolutions that are contrary to God's Will. However, we're often not mindful of the fact that God might have had a miraculous plan for delivering us, had we not endeavored to ditch these hurdles.

In neglecting to present our difficulties to the Lord and to trust Him to work for us in accordance with His Will, we may very well forfeit an ordained miraculous intervention that he planned for us to cross over that very hurdle. Had not the Israelites consulted the Lord and yielded to His directions, they would have never experienced the parting of the Red Sea.

God's strength and power is vividly manifested, not when everything in our life is already intact, but in the presence of our difficulties. Trying though your circumstances may be, be reminded that you cannot be healed unless you are impaired. You will never experience a single miracle unless there is first a predicament. When faced with our dilemmas, wouldn't it be worthy to therefore seek to endure and trust the Lord to intercede on our behalf as He sees fit?

Blessed is that person who endures trials, because it is through them that he shall receive the crown of life which the Lord has promised to those who love Him (James 1:12). Watching, praying and feasting on God's promises empower us to endure difficulties and resist temptations.

Whatever situation you experience, be reminded of the promises of God. Never forget His power, His might, His faithfulness and His goodness towards you. While God does not divinely ordain all difficulties, He does allow them into the lives of His Children for specific reasons. Trust Him to either deliver you from them or to journey with you through them. Whatever the unique reason(s) for them in your life, always be mindful that God intends that His name should be glorified.

It's so very important to learn to accept God's way, even if it is not packaged with the colorful wrappers that you adore. With God, the gift is often more pricey than the wrapping paper. Your difficulties are nothing more than wrapping papers. Beneath the wrappers are precious gems that God desires to impart to you - all wrapped up! Why reject a precious gift just because the wrapper is unsightly? By ditching your difficulties, you also ditch God's gifts to you – true virtues that He intends to impart to your life.

Your present suffering is incomparable to the virtues that God desires to mold in you, through it (Romans 8:18). Choose to persevere. A helpful reminder is that God will never give you more than you can bear. In fact, with God, all things are possible for you. There is absolutely nothing that is unbearable - nothing that the least of His Children cannot endure or gain victory over while journeying in His presence.

Chapter 8

Withstand & Stand Tall

This chapter will focus on being victorious over challenging situations that often seek to interfere with our relationship with God and consequently rob us of the joy and fulfillment that He desires for us to experience. As you Journey with God, take care not to allow these, or anything, to deprive you of experiencing to its fullest, the Essence of Life's Journey.

When God Delays or Says "No"

There is the concept that God doesn't say no. What loving parent would not say no to a child who, out of naivety, constantly requests candies because they taste sweet in the mouth, not knowing they are also bitter for the tummy? A wise and loving parent would act in the interest of their child's wellbeing. When the desires of the child conflicts with his welfare then out of love, that parent must say no and seek to enlighten the child concerning what is really best for him.

Our omniscient God knows better than we do. We must surrender to Him our will. We therefore have to be willing to work with His Will instead of insisting and expecting that He works with ours.

It is important that we allow our loving Father to mold into our character and wisdom: new eyes to discern His Will, a new mind to understand them and a new heart to appreciate them. God allows our turmoil or may delay to intervene, not because He's distant from the situation, or distant from our pain and hurt. But only because He envisions victories for us that can only be accomplished through suffering.

After consulting with the Lord three times concerning a weakness that Paul earnestly wanted to be removed from his life, the Lord replied: "My grace is sufficient for you: for my strength is made perfect in weaknesses."

Kayan Smith

Paul continued: "Most gladly therefore will I rather glory in my infirmities that the power of Christ may rest upon me. Therefore, I take pleasure in infirmities, in reproaches, in necessities, in persecutions, in distresses for Christ's sake: for when I am weak, then am I strong" (2 Corinthians 12:9&10).

When you're at your lowest, weakest point, it is the greatest opportunity for God to manifest His power and His might into your life. He may not turn back the hands of time. He may not erase a mistake. He may not respond how and when you desire. He may not take you away from the problem either. But He will give you all the strength that you need to endure and to be an over-comer.

Your new life in Christ, will determine to a great extent your perception and appreciation of God's choice of interventions in your life. This will empower you to allow the joy of the Lord to abound in your heart, even through difficulties. In your renewed state, your greatest challenges will now become most remarkable and memorable because you will be left with no doubt that God was present and nothing but His strength brought you through.

After Lazarus' family sent the news to Christ that Lazarus, who Christ loves dearly, is sick, Christ delayed (St John 11). He delayed until four days after it was seemingly too late - Lazarus had died. What pain, what discouragement, what disappointment must have overwhelmed Lazarus's sisters? They called on their Lord because they were confident that he could have healed Lazarus, but he chose not to.

There are times when you may honestly feel like people have failed you, life has failed you, even God has failed you. You called and He hasn't responded. You look around and see others call, for even less urgent situation than yours and He doesn't delay. You, on the other hand, seek Him earnestly on a significant issue and He delays.

Christ was busy ministering to the needs of others while he delayed in attending to Lazarus' needs. Four days, four long days after Lazarus' death, Christ responded to the call. Yet he didn't show up absent-minded and detached from the situation. To the contrary - He wept! God feels our pain. Despite the delay, He feels your pain.

In the moment of the heavy cloud of darkness that surrounds you, you may not sense His presence through the darkest and lowest points in your life, but He hasn't abandoned you. He grieves when you grieve. The Savior was

124 | Withstand & Stand Tall

touched by the death of Lazarus. He is touched with your feelings too. He is moved by your laughter; and your pain, hurt, and anguish which cannot be adequately explained and expressed to your closest mortal friends. He knows your pain. He mourns with you, and He understands. He longs to comfort you.

When Christ asked for the gravestones to be removed from around Lazarus' grave, Martha was stunned and replied that Lazarus's body must now stink, after all its now 4 days since his death. Christ's reminder to her was "Have I not said to you, that, if you would believe, you will see the glory of God?"(John 11: 40). Is Christ reminding you of this today? If you will believe you will see the glory of God in whatever situation you face. Martha believed and indeed God was glorified through the resurrection of Lazarus.

There will be situations where God wants to work miracles in your life. And when He does, you will experience the fulfillment that comes with living in accordance with His Will. He yearns to rescue you through His power and His might - but you must believe! You must allow Him to do for you and even through you, what's necessary. Martha tried to intervene when she thought a decaying body was too much for Christ to handle, but His reminder quieted her.

The One who is the resurrection and the life (John 11:25), who will on the Resurrection Day raise innumerable bodies that have laid dead for thousands of years is more than able to raise a man dead 4 days. Let not unbelief interfere with the manifestation of God's power and presence in your life. Let it not hinder His Will for you. If God can raise the dead, what can't He do for living? What can't He do for you who are already alive?

Like the rest of us, I've had my own experiences of God saying no. I once consulted the Lord about a matter of deep significance. I had so many questions. I surrendered the issue to the Lord and He delayed, until the situation worsened. I couldn't understand why? How could God have let me down when I have placed my life, my faith, my all in His hands? Why hasn't He given me a favorable response? I felt so helpless. I felt like a child who could not swim, yet casted in the deep ocean without a life-jacket or a boat and no land insight… I so felt the need for a miraculous deliverance.

I pleaded to the Lord, to at least teach me to swim or even show me the way out. I poured my heart out to the Lord for Him to remove the situation - and He answered, "No".

Instead, that moment, God gave me the greatest assurance that I needed. With great disappointment, He offers even greater assurance. At my midnight, God did not teach me how to swim, neither did he provide me a life jacket or boat, or even tossed me on dry land. In other words, He did not remove my difficulties or take me away from them.

My Heavenly Father empowered me to walk on the troubled water. He gave me peace in the presence of my turbulence. He gave me victory in the midst of my battle. He replenished His joy in me in the middle of my depressing crisis. He restored my hope in Him when there was nothing tangible surrounding my situation to hope in.

God said "no" to my request because His Plan was greater than I could have envisioned during the situation. Looking back today I'm tremendously grateful that He said no. In saying no, He turned my tears into laughter, my mourning into eternal joy. God brought me to a place where it was plainly visible that ultimately, nothing in this world really matters as long as I am in His presence.

With His reassurance, everything - all my cares and desires - became so secondary, so minor, that they were basically non-existent. In that moment, nothing besides the presence of God absorbed my mind and my being. My request, in fact, even my dilemma, was incomparable to what God had to offer. I was granted the peaceful, joyful, comforting atmosphere of the presence of my Lord and Savior and in the middle of my difficulty I was reassured that everything would be ok - and indeed, it was so.

When God decides not to grant your desires how you want and when you want, it's often because He desires to:

- have His Will, and not yours, fulfilled in your life
- teach you valuable lesson(s) about Himself, yourself and life
- glorify His name for the sake of unbelievers
- draw you closer to Him in prayer, and/or
- mold into you virtues such as patience, faith, acceptance and complete dependence on Him

Martha believed Lazarus would have been raised the resurrection day, but never envisioned that it would have happened right there and then, 4 days after his death. Like in the case of Martha, Christ's Plan for you is even more glorious than your human mind can now conceive. To claim this Plan starts by believing it, even if you don't completely understand. It starts by believing it, even when God delays or says no to your wishes.

Next time you present an issue to the Lord, why not trust for Him to work in accordance with His Will and not yours. How much this will free you from undue stress and anxiety so that the joy of the Lord may abound in your heart.

Between a Rock and a Hard Place

You might find yourself in a crisis where you seemingly cannot move forward, backward or even stand still because your enemy or dilemma appears to be closing in on you. How much these situations seek to rob us from the contentment we have found in Christ.

What a dilemma the Israelites experienced as soon as they excitedly left Egypt for the glorious Promised Land (Exodus 14). Before them was the Red Sea and chasing behind was the Egyptian army. They were being closed in by death, whether they chose to go forward, turn back or even stay still. Or at least, so it seemed.

"Fear not, *stand still* and see the salvation of the Lord which he will show to you today," commanded Moses, "because the Egyptians who you have seen today, you shall see them no more forever."

With that command the Israelites stood still as Moses sought the Lord on their behalf. The Lord commanded that they move forward. The same God who lead them to the Red Sea, lead them through it - walking on dry land. The adversary before them was subdued by the power of the God who was directing their Path.

As the parted sea paved their way forward, God re-positioned the visible representation of His presence behind them to offer assurance of His protection from their pursuing enemy. As a protective element God stood between the Egyptians and the Israelites so that the two were never in contact. The Egyptians, at their best attempt, could not close in on the Israelites. The Israelites' Guide was like a cloud of darkness to the Egyptians while being a guiding light to them. The enemies behind were confounded only to be later destroyed.

As the Egyptians pursued the Israelites through the Red Sea, the Lord allowed the sea to regain its composure after the Israelites crossed over. All the Egyptians behind them, including Pharaoh and his army, were destroyed within the sea.

The Lord can and will fight your battles if you allow Him to. Why not allow Him to be your refuge and strength. He is a very present help in trouble (Psalm 46:1). Like the Israelites, stand still and listen to the directives of your Lord. Find peace, contentment and safety under His leadership. When it seems there is danger moving forward, backward or even in standing still, He will cause the enemies surrounding you to vanish at His command. He will direct your Path for you to move forward towards His intended destination.

Being between the rock and the hard place can be nothing more than a temporary fixture when you're journeying with Christ. You must move forward. Ahead are giants to be conquered, battles to be won and victories to be celebrated.

Nothing can stand in your way and keep you behind forever - maybe a seasonal set-back, but never permanent set-back, because you are on a Journey. You are on God's ordained Journey to a better place. You are destined towards a better life spiritually and in all the areas of life that God envisions for you. God desires for you to exploit the joy and blessings of the life that He has guided you into.

You must conquer as you advance into that promised life, right here in this lifetime, and to the Promised Land. You must seek to move forward even when in the middle of a depressing crisis that might confront you in this life. But first, stand still. Stand still and seek God's direction. Then you will see the saving power and goodness of the Lord towards you in your own situation between the rock and the hard place.

Journeying Ahead of the Closed Door

God often uses situations and circumstances to communicate His Will to us. Therefore, instead of allowing the trying situations to rob us of our peace of mind and contentment, we should always seek to discern God's Will through them.

Sometimes God allows doors to close in our faces in order to open new doors of opportunities and blessings for us. When God closes or allows a door to close before you, it obviously means that the best that He desires for you is not behind that door. Regardless of how glamorous that closed door appears God envisions better. So, stop looking at the closed door and be focused on your Guide.

God might close doors of opportunities for you as a means of commanding you to wait on Him. He might be prompting you to seek to discern His direction for your life. This might very well be His way of calling you into a more intimate relationship with Him where His directives become clearer to you and you are better prepared to embark on a new phase of your journey with Him. Therefore, instead of drowning in disappointment and despair, it is so important to seek to learn God's Will.

A closed door may also mean that God is indicating to you that He desires for you to abandon your own way for His. Often He has to shed things from our lives to capture our attention. By closing doors of opportunities that you envision, God may just be trying to open your eyes to that glorious Plan that He desires to replace with yours.

Sometimes, that closed door may even be an indication that God desires for you to take a step forward as His Plan for you heightens. He closes the door behind you so that you don't find comfort in remaining stationary or turning back but remain focused on where He is directing you.

After the Israelites passed through the parted Red Sea, it closed up behind them. This not only destroyed their enemies but also prevented them from returning to Egypt when confronted with difficulties as they journeyed towards their designated destination. The path behind them was already sealed up. Their most feasible choice was now to look ahead and move forward.

To encourage her maturing little ones to fly, the mother eagle would terminate her routine of returning with food to the nest. Instead, she would leave the food nearby on the branch that the nest is built on. Or she would perch outside of the nest with the food in her beak. Otherwise, her babies may never attempt to leave the comfort of their nest to explore the vast, beautiful world. Otherwise, they might never sense the desire to soar above the nest, above the tree and beyond the clouds, to unknown heights that they cannot even glimpse from their hiding place in the nest.

As they feed daily, soon they begin to outgrow the nest. The nest is only intended to host and nurture them for a time - until they mature and are prepared to embark on a higher phase of their life. The same goes for you.

What is your nest? Is God closing the door to that nest? Rather than remain in despair, pursue the vast opportunities outside of that nest. Otherwise, you will miss out on opportunities to glorify God and opportunities to explore and enjoy the bounties beyond that nest. As you grow and mature, the nest becomes too small for you - or to be precise, you outgrow the nest. When you do not recognize God's promptings for you to explore something higher and vaster than that nest, God will remove either you or it, as a precursor to attaining greater.

We cannot see the invisible. We cannot predict the future. We often do not embrace change when we're already comfortable. We are not certain of what lurks behind a new situation so it is reassuring to clench to the former or the present. Sometimes the only way that God can release that grip is to remove whatever it is that we are clenching on to.

For God to open our minds to embrace changes that He desires to flow into our lives, He often has to remove the 'comforter(s)' from our lives. If we don't get cold we may never feel the need to seek warmth. Exposing us to the cold is one way of helping us to see and reach for the opened door before us. If God allows a door to close in your life, it's only because He has already opened another for you. Why stare at the closed door instead of searching for the opened one?

You are on a Journey. Doors will always be shutting and opening in your life as long as you're going to move from one stage in life to another. It's just a natural phenomenon of life's Journey. It's never easy to let go and move on but you must if you're to rise above where you presently are and live more abundantly.

Sometimes you may have to journey through tunnels, to transit from the closed door to the opened door; very dark tunnels - difficult times in your Journey. But, seek to always find hope in Christ, even when it seem like it's the very end of the road in your life. In Christ, it's only the end of one chapter. The end of one chapter of your life marks the beginning of another. Before every closed door is the Lord, waiting to guide you into a new, more glorious chapter of your life.

In Times of Grief or Loss

Moments of great loss can make us feel powerless and reluctant to go on.

Maybe you have lost a loved one, a job, a cherished relationship or something of great significance to your life. Because of this loss you might feel incapable of ever being able to be a joyful person and live a fulfilling life. Deep down inside, you may not even have the will power to do so either. It's never easy to rise above the emptiness of a great loss and look ahead. The impulse to grieve a loss is perhaps as natural and involuntary as even blinking.

But, as you grieve seek opportunities to cope with and manage your grief. Fundamentally, find comfort in feasting continuously on the promises of God in the Scripture. Maybe you can also try journaling where you spill out your feelings just as they are. Or, writing letters specifically to God; trying creative expressions like fine arts; confiding in close spiritual friends; join a grief group with Christians who share similar loss; or seek professional support from a Christian councilor. But never seek to ignore or suppress your grief as a means of moving forward. Instead, seek positive and helpful ways to express your emotions.

We grieve differently, for different length of time and respond uniquely as we seek to cope. It is important to be patient with yourself. Do not become frustrated if your efforts towards healing fail to quickly mature into your recovery. Instead, be grateful for even the tiniest blessings and break-through.

There will be moments when you feel you cannot make it even past the next few minutes but when you trust God He will empower you to make it through those minutes - and even hours, days, weeks, months and years. And it will get better with the passing moments, despite re-bounds.

Sometimes it's very difficult and even appears to be impossible to appreciate and accept any good arising from our loss. For instance, there seems to never be any basis for the acceptance of the loss of a loved one. For this reason, I've heard a man shared that he refuses to become a Christian because he cannot see how a loving God could allow His Only Begotten Son to die as described in the Bible. "Which loving parent would allow that?" He questioned.

But we do not see as God sees. His thoughts and ways are not ours (Isaiah 55:8&9). Our understanding is so limited in comparison to His unlimited wisdom. God has revealed to us why His Son had to die. Therefore, as Christians, though we grieve Christ's death we have come to appreciate and accept it. However, there are losses in our personal lives that we may never understand any justifiable reason for. Our faith must therefore rise above the loss, above the pain and the grief that seek to engulf us, to that place where we find confidence in the reality that the Lord knows best.

Your loss may be merely a consequence of the sin-tainted imperfect world that we live in. Never-the-less, God wants to refine you as a result of this loss. He also desires for you to find perfect peace and comfort in His arms right here in this life and even in your troubled situation. He wants you to find refuge in Him. He wants you to experience His joyful presence even as you grieve.

Nothing works better than trusting in God. While mechanisms can help you to cope with and manage your grief, only the Lord can empower you to be an over-comer.

The birds will still chirp and the flowers will still bloom, whether or not you choose to acknowledge their beauty. Never forget that God has blessed you with the amazing gift of life. Why not allow God to soothe your grief so that you can be able to still enjoy the beauty of life while you have life?

Blessed are those who mourn because they shall be comforted (Matthew 5:4). This is Christ's promise to his followers. You are being comforted. Accepting a great loss or specifically, the loss of loved ones does not mean that you forget them. Rather, it signifies that you are being comforted. It means that Christ's promise is being fulfilled in you. Grief is culminated by acceptance of our loss. Trust God to take you to this goal as you seize the joy of the Lord.

When You Feel Victimized

It is so very hard for us to move beyond the negative impact of pain and suffering that has been inflicted on our lives by others. However, while we didn't choose to become victims, we do choose whether or not we will remain one. In choosing to remain a victim we grant our offenders and/or our negative predicament unlimited power over our lives. Moving forward will never be easy but it's the best decision. It is the only way we can truly step into that new life with Christ and truly journey with him.

Most, if not all of us, have been a victim of someone or something. For some of us, our dilemma and the impact of our pain is more overwhelming than for others. We're all unique and so is the effect of our situations on us.

Our pain is unique. No one, but God, knows the impact like we do. That's right - God knows and He has the cure. His holy presence provides the essence of all that we need in this life. This should be our focus whenever we feel victimized. Healing is not only possible but it is also available for all of us, despite the nature or magnitude of what we have experienced.

The choice is ours. Our choice will determine the quality of life that we allow God to bestow on us. You do have the power of choice. You have the power to choose between remaining bound by the shackles of your past predicament or to walk freely and fully into the better Way that is provided for you through Christ. Why not choose to allow yourself that better chance in life. Why not choose to be free to live the joyful and fulfilling life that God is bestowing on you.

God wants to unleash the richness of His Life into your life. He longs to rid you of shackles that have impaired your life and held you captive. He longs to set you free, free to walk into the fullness of the new life that He has reserved just for you. Allow Him to deliver you from anything that has held you captive emotionally, physically or even spiritually and have impaired your life.

God provides the essence of your being. His wisdom, power, love and compassion surpass your situation. They surpass any situation that you can ever experience. He is now imparting to your life all that is needed for you to rise up, overcome and live victoriously.

Our life experiences will either break us or make us, based on the direction of influence that we allow them to have on us and our lives. Why not allow God to recreate you into a better person, despite and even through these experiences. Why not allow Him to redirect and thoroughly replenish your life.

To please God in all things and to live the joyful and fulfilling life that He has granted you, you must choose to allow Him to channel even the most negative experiences in your life, into a positive direction. Allow Him to channel them into the direction that shapes you into a better person and your Path into one of triumph.

Trading in Anger for Joy

One morning at work my attention was attracted to a violent outburst from a client. The client related a complaint that the receptionist was unpleasant to him. The receptionist testified to treating him in the same pleasant manner as all the other clients; however, she apologized to him over and over for the fact that he perceived that impression of her behavior. The client was still dissatisfied and refused to accept the apology.

Instead, he insisted, "She was treating me like I'm unimportant". I queried the words she used in conveying this message. He replied: "She's treating me like she can do without my money and I'm paying just like everyone else". I joined the receptionist in apologizing to him and expressed my regret that he had such an unpleasant encounter.

With that he basically exploded, refusing the apology and demanding that someone fires the receptionist. Then he continued about the need for justice. It was now clear in my mind that the problem obviously started before he entered the office so I gently sat him down and asked, "What really is the matter? You don't seem to be in a good mood today". For the first time, he paused, kept a calm composure and then replied, "I'm an angry person - a very angry man."

When we view the world through angry eyes, everything looks different. The people we interact with look different; even the flowers in their full glory look dreary and miserable. Life on a whole looks different. Simple things become a bother and the best of life becomes tainted, dimmed, undermined and taken for granted. In anger, we just don't see the world and life as they are. We don't see people or situations as they are either. Anger often takes away the joy, the humor - the blessings out of life.

After experiencing a bitter break-up, a friend once confided in me that anger is very addictive. And it is true. When angry, we often find consolation in remaining in an angry state, instead of trying to break free from it. To some extent, this form of consolation comes from the false idea that being angry is a kind of retribution towards the person or situation that upsets us. However, remaining angry has no good reward. In fact, the person holding a grudge will most likely experience the dreadful impact from doing so.

The mind, body and soul of an angry person become scarred by anger. In an angry state our minds become emotionally clouded and we don't think with clarity or make rational decisions. No wonder in an angry state we may feel as though we have the right to remain angry and may very well choose to exercise that right. But that's one right we don't have to exercise.

The longer we remain angry, the greater the negative impact on us because we shun the peaceful, joyful presence of God from our lives. This robs us of the joy and peace of mind needed to properly nourish our being. Anger is a negative emotion which has negative repercussions on not only the angry person, but his relationships with others. It is therefore godly not to nurture bitter feelings but seek to overcome them and manage our emotions.

We will always be confronted with unpleasant people or circumstances that will cause pain, hurt and set-backs in our lives. When we waste our time and energy on festering anger we never see the need to forgive. Our relationships suffer and so does our life. We make decisions that often damage our own interests, for the sake of being vindictive or 'making statements'. We miss opportunities to learn practical life lessons, to grow in Christ and to share his love with others.

Something we have discussed from Chapter 2 is that God does not force Himself and His way on us. We cannot cherish negative, resentful or hateful thoughts and emotions while asking God to empower our lives, or even expecting Him to empower us to overcome anger. We must be willing to completely abandon our old way – even our cherished negative emotions and negative way of thinking. This will facilitate the environment for God to thoroughly renew our minds.

Instead of holding on to anger from the past, wouldn't it be better to:

1. Admit your anger

2. Look for the good in others and the blessings in your life (regardless of how horrible people treat you or how horrible your life may appear to be). Write them down if necessary.

3. Be mindful of your own flaws and meditate on the reality that God did not angrily reject you because of these flaws. Instead He loved you and forgave you. He covenants to save you at the greatest cost ever and to restore your relationship with Him. Others also need to experience this kind of love and forgiving attitude from you, towards them.

4. Admit that though you have been hurt you inflict greater hurt on yourself (and maybe unnecessary hurt on others) by choosing to remain angry.

5. Ask yourself: "Who and/or what have hurt my life and severely angered me?" Surrender them, all of them; all your cherished pain, hurt, vengeance and anger to God and trust Him to heal you. Believe that what He has to offer is far greater than

clinging to an angry, unforgiving heart. Consider it done. Claim His rewards!

We're not living in a perfect world. In the future you will encounter upsetting situations. God will not just miraculously prevent you from experiencing the emotion of anger all together. He would rather impart to you the continued presence of His Holy Spirit in you, to empower you to rise above these situations when they next present themselves.

Therefore, as the situation pops up why not silently, in that very instant, ask the Lord how He is working in that situation to manage your emotions and empower you to overcome anger. It might also be helpful to be conscious of your emotions. Instead of becoming out of control, ensure that you allow the Lord to be in control of your emotions. Think before you act. Ask the Lord to direct your thoughts, emotions and actions instantaneously. Act in a manner that glorifies God and is in the best interest of all concerned.

Allow God to recreate your mind, emotions and entire being according to His righteousness. In doing this, when you are angered you will not sin. You will be empowered to get pass this anger even before the day is passed. You would not have given any place for the devil in your heart and mind. (Ephesians 4:23-27). You would not have been robbed of basking in the joyful and fulfilling life that comes only from finding solace in God.

Letting Go of Insecurity & Fear of Failure

It is a fact that everybody's life is lacking in some area or another. Insecurity arises not just from having these unmet needs and desires, but from becoming pre-occupied with them. We suffer from insecurity when our faith is not firmly built on the solid Foundation that is unconditional and eternal. God is a sure Foundation for all times and faith in Him is the only key to the rich treasures of salvation, wisdom and knowledge (Isaiah 33:6).

On the other hand, people leave our lives – one way or another. A good job and stable financial status may not always accompany us throughout life. Outward beauty fades and becomes distorted. There will always be persons more talented and intellectual, at least in some areas, than each of us. Happy circumstances sometimes change for the worst. Building our security on fluctuating circumstances like these, perishable objects and fallible people like ourselves is no different from building our homes on quicksand.

While we may not all find security in the things of this world, there are those of us who have no greater confidence in the power and goodness of God towards us. Being faithless is no less destructive as having misplaced faith. The key to overcoming any form of insecurity is to first find our security in Christ and allow his presence in our lives to displace our insufficiencies.

At times God will prevent us from attaining a particular goal on our agenda, allow us to lose something significant to our lives, or allow us to even fail at our plans, as a means of exposing to us our innate weakness, vulnerability and need for Him - all for the ultimate purpose of anchoring our confidence firmly in Him. So when confronted by our lack and even set-backs, our focus should be diverted to finding security in God.

When we focus on our weaknesses and deficiencies and compare them with the strengths and assets of others we will automatically feel insecure. A rule of thumb is never to compare you to others. If comparison doesn't make you insecure, chances are it will make you haughty.

God endows all of us with a unique set of strengths mingled with weaknesses. Each person's strength should compensate for the other person's weakness. That is what God intends. Not for us to live and operate as a whole to ourselves but to live and work together as a complete body, whether in our families, neighborhoods, workplace or church.

Instead of coveting the strengths of others, identify your own strengths and ways of complementing them with those you collaborate with. What cannot be accomplished through you as an individual is intended to be accomplished as a group. Instead of being in despair about your weakness, celebrate your strengths and the strengths of others. You celebrate your strengths by using them meaningfully to glorify God. You celebrate the strengths of others by cheerfully allowing them to employ their skills and talents to their greatest potential.

If God impresses a new project or venture on your heart, never allow insecurity or fear of failure to hold you back. Embark on it with boldness until its completion. Such great fulfillment this will unleash into your life. Yet, you might be afraid of the opinions of others. "What will people say or think? Will they ridicule, gossip about it, or oppose me? Will they think and say I can't do it and just wait around to see me fail?"

They might. However, if by carrying out your God-ordained, probably once-in-a-lifetime objective you experience reproach, wouldn't it be worth it after all? You might even earn some well-warranted criticisms from mistakes along the way but that's all part of the process.

It's never easy coming out of our comfort zone but to really live the fulfilling life, we must. We will experience many failures before we get it right - that is, for those of us who are normal. Just like a toddler learning to walk, you will have a few falls, bumps and bruises but with each fall comes greater understanding of how to stand up straight while firmly moving ahead.

Babies don't consciously sit around and never get up because they fell or because of the fear of falling. Instead, they usually get up with great enthusiasm to try again. What then of us who are more advanced in our intellect and our abilities? Shouldn't we too embark on whatever ventures God has impressed on our hearts and has invested in us to accomplish?

When we choose to be laid-back and excuse ourselves from living life to the fullest potential invested in us we commit suicide on the life we were born to live - we're technically alive, but practically dead. What better attempt to rob ourselves of the joy and fulfillment that God offers.

God has endowed you with a unique life and unique gifts and abilities to share with the world through service. Do not allow insecurities, fear of failure, anything or anyone to prevent this from happening.

When you recognize any disabilities or weaknesses in you, allow God to use you to glorify Himself through them. Identify your gifts and abilities and allow the Lord to direct you in using them to serve Him. When you triumph, in spite of your weaknesses and disabilities, the resulting inspiration on your own life and the life of others will be nothing less than marvelous.

Alone and Loneliness

One thing that those who travel on the Narrow Road of life have in common is that spiritually, we journey with only a few others whose lives are consistent with God's Calling. For this reason we may encounter just a few persons, and sometimes no one, in our workplaces and even our homes who share common life interests, goals and mission as we do.

You can become spiritually isolated in a regular crowd, if the path of other members of your crowd just doesn't intertwine with yours. For some people, being alone in this sense often results in feelings of loneliness.

Generally, as humans, our lives can become lonely for diverse reasons, such as: losing a loved one, relocating to somewhere new, making lifestyle changes such as becoming a Christian, having an impaired social life – and, the list goes on...

Be reminded that hurtful, painful relationships can be eagerly born from loneliness. When we become too desperate for friends we might be led to form close bonds with people who do not add to a healthy Christian friendship. The fact that they satisfy our loneliness during the initial stages of the interaction causes us to latch on to them too quickly, and then become hurt just as quickly. Think logically and rationally about forming interactions with others out of feelings of loneliness. Instead, be guided, not by your feelings but, by God's wisdom.

Closer Relationship with God

Loneliness is not just a result of inadequate amount of people in our lives to interact with. Rather, it is a result of an inadequate level of desired and needed interaction and intimate bond. Therefore, it is not the number of friendships that we have that really matters; but the quality of the relationships. So the answer to our loneliness may not be in building more relationships but, in building deeper relationships.

These feelings of loneliness may be prompted by unfulfilled relationships with fellow humans or with God. We should allow God to help us to distinguish this difference and to fulfill this need accordingly. If you find yourself seeking longingly for someone to fill a void in your life that you doubt any ordinary person can ever fill – it is quite likely that who you are truly seeking after is Christ. In this case, you must seek to find fulfillment through a deeper walk with him.

There are times too when God will shed objects and people from our lives as a means of binding us closer to Him in preparation for the unfolding of His great plans for us. We can become so occupied with our own goals and in our associations with others that the level of undisturbed intimacy that God desires to achieve with us is hardly possible.

If necessary, God will bring you through a season of solitude where you can hear His voice more audibly. His Will becomes clearer and you are more receptive to be molded by Him. This is seen in the lives of many Bible characters that experienced seasons of solitude before embarking on an exalted phase in God's Plan for their lives.

God called Abraham away from his country and extended family to live in a country that he did not know and among people who most likely didn't even speak his language (Genesis 12:1-6). But in doing this, God had a great Plan to produce a pure religion through isolating Abraham from his people and country of origin.

Moses was prepared to lead God's people only after spending many years in isolation from these, his own people (Exodus 2-4).

Joseph was empowered by God to rule over Egypt after being separated from his family, sold as a slave and wrongfully imprisoned for years (Genesis 37 & 39-41).

After Christ's baptism, the Holy Spirit led him in the wilderness for 40 days, surrounded by wild beasts and temptation from the devil (Mark 1:12). His Heavenly Father was with him, and during this period of solitude God prepared him for a steeper phase of his ordained ministry.

Careful reflection has made me realize that it is during my own seasons of solitude that the Holy Spirit's presence and influence in my own life has been most remarkable. These are the periods when God's directives for my life are usually most vividly revealed. For this reason, my seasons of solitude feel nothing less than sacred.

Always be reminded that you are never alone - God is always with you. His Spirit dwells in you. God can empower you to be in solitude and not be lonely. He allows you to experience periods of solitude for a divine reason.

If you feel you are isolated from interacting with others on a level that you desire, trust that God might be using this opportunity to prepare you for greater things ahead. Instead of allowing loneliness to interject God's divine Will, find companionship in drawing closer to Him and being immersed into His presence.

Closer Relationship with Others

Feelings of loneliness may also be like a psychological alarm clock that is, not only indicating that your social needs are unmet but is also, prompting you to seek closer interactions with others. Take time to consult the Lord concerning how to go about meeting these needs. Be open to His guidance. Use your initiative. One way of creating interactions with people of similar interests as yours is becoming active in your church and community, within groups of your interest.

Trust the Lord to provide for your social needs. It is not His intention for you to journey alone. When God created Eve as a companion for Adam, He did so from the recognition of Adam's need for interaction with someone like himself (Genesis 2:20-23). If you feel a void in your life for a companion, friends or family, just as in the case of Adam, the Lord sees this need and it shall be fulfilled– one way or the other, in accordance with His perfect wisdom.

Trust God to fill that void with that person or people whose lives and goals are in accordance with His Will, so that together you can find deep interaction with Him. The focal point of every profound, fulfilling, unending and joyful human relationship is established on and preserved only through God. The sovereignty of God over our lives is applicable to every single aspect of our being and every aspect of our lives – even in enriching our relationships with others.

Persecution, Disappointment & Suffering for Christ's Sake

Often we're encouraged that our most pleasant and happiest days on this earth are ahead and not behind us, causing us to hope in future events on this earth, instead of in God's goodness and faithfulness. But, shouldn't the Christian's hope be anchored on something greater than the idea of temporal bliss beyond our calamities while we journey on earth?

In subtle ways such thinking teaches us to find hope in our circumstances, not in Christ. Rather, let us hope in the reality that regardless of whatever befalls us throughout our lifetime, when our lives are in God's hands, our lives have great value, meaning and purpose. This is because our life's mission and our contentment is not limited to or defined by our circumstances in this life.

It is one thing to glorify God in good times, but it's another to glorify Him through persecution, disappointment and great suffering – even to the end. This speaks of the power and authenticity of God's re-creative work in us.

Persecution and suffering

Persecution might hardly sound like a fitting topic to talk about these days, yet it's a very relevant topic for all those who have seriously decided to Journey on the Narrow Road. Persecution is a natural consequence of following Christ (2 Timothy 3:12). As a follower of Christ, your presence and principles will create offense to those who choose to live contrary to the testimony of Jesus Christ. Therefore, you must not lose hope and confidence over God's sovereignty in your life when this happens.

Christ warned us assuredly that if he was persecuted then so will those who follow him (John 15: 20). It is the tears, sweat and blood of Christ that paved the Christian's pathway – your pathway even. Many true followers of Christ have dared to walk the complete pathway and stand for God at all cost, including their very lives.

Majority of Christ's 12 disciples were martyred. John, the son of Zebedee, was thrown into boiling oil but escaped death. Is it therefore shocking if you too are persecuted for Christ's sake?

Being faithful to God may have repercussions that include being hated, isolated, falsely accused, threatened and sabotaged. Nevertheless, when you choose to follow Christ all the way you must follow him up on the mountain top, down in the valley and even to the cross, if that is where he leads. Be reminded, Christ and many others have travelled this Path before you. God is with you.

It's so important to be careful not to become disoriented and confused by such sufferings. The real purpose and significance of your life lies deeper than the surface of how blissful or troubled the *circumstances* of your life's Journey. Having God's presence with us and His divine Will fulfilled in our lives is the deciding factor of whether we are experiencing the Essence of Life's Journey. This determines the measure of the life that we live.

This is evidenced in the life of John the Baptist, who Christ declared that among those born of women - there is no greater (Matthew 11:11). What could have been so outstanding about someone's life that the very Son of God himself made such an exalted declaration? John the Baptist wore clothes made from camel's hair and he fed on locusts and wild honey (Matthew 3:4). There is really nothing about this lowly kind of life to be admired, is there?

What sets John's life on a pedestal is the fulfillment of God's mission for his life. John was born for the purpose of proclaiming the presence of the Messiah among the people of his day. What an awesome responsibility!

John's mission was even prophesied well in advance of his birth by the Prophet Isaiah (Matthew 3:3). For many years John preached the gospel, inviting people to accept Christ, repent and be baptized. He baptized many. He never worked a single miracle, never performed any spectacular act; but he openly spoke the simple truth about the Savior and the Savior's mission. For that reason, many believed in Christ (John 10:41 &42).

John the Baptist was eventually imprisoned after he reproved Herod for marrying Herodias, his brother's wife (Mark 6:17). John was later beheaded at the request of unforgiving Herodias (Mark 6:21-26).

What a way to live and what a way to die. Yet his life was glorious and so was his death. God's awesome purpose for John's life was fulfilled. His death, though seemingly tragic was nothing less than a victorious end.

John's death marked the climax of a life here on earth that was dedicated to fulfilling God's Will and glorifying God from start to finish. His life and death was a complete sacrifice made to the work of the Lord. His life was not dictated by his own desires or will, but the Lord's. This is evident even by his death. He was substantially fuelled and driven by the Holy Spirit. He experienced the Essence of Life in its full measure. No wonder he is the greatest born among women.

Have you ever stopped to wonder when Christ looks at your life, what is his declaration? Are you daily allowing His Will or yours to govern your life?

Disappointment

The Good News or the gospel just doesn't seem so good to us when it is mingled with what appears to be disappointing truths. However, unless we find rest in Christ and learn to appreciate and accept all that comes with following after him, we can never truly enter into and abide in the joy of the Lord.

We will all encounter disappointments at some point in our Journey. When this happens, it is comforting to be reminded that all things do work together for good to those who love God and are called according to His purpose (Romans 8:28). Some chapters in your life's Journey may seem to be bad, but when assembled into God's great Plan for your life, they work towards good. They work towards a greater purpose that we may never fully grasp or appreciate while we endure them.

After John the Baptist was imprisoned, he never believed that the end of his life would occur behind prison bars. After all, wasn't he the one who prepared the way for the Messiah to be accepted by the people? Wasn't the Messiah still alive and well with power and glory that the Father has bestowed on him?

John lingered behind the prison walls day after day, awaiting that special visit from Christ – His Savior and Deliverer. However, that visitor never came. What disappointment John must have experienced. The Person, who he spent his entire life representing, was somewhat absent to represent him when he wanted to be rescued from the bondage of his prison walls.

John spent his life building the people's hope and faith in Christ, yet behind those walls he sent the question to Christ: "Are you the One that should come, or should we look for another?" (Matthew 11:3).

That question clearly revealed that this single disappointment placed on trial the belief system, on which hanged John's entire life ministry. There were intricacies about Christ's ministry that John didn't fully understand at the time, yet he surrendered his entire life in support of this ministry. However, it is important to note that John's question to Christ was meant to confirm his belief in Christ and to dispel his doubt - not the reverse of this.

What are the prison walls in your life? Whatever disappointment they might have caused, let these walls strengthen, and not shatter, your belief system and your willingness for God's Will to be done in your life.

Regardless of whether the Journey gets disappointing and rough, do not lose faith. When there seems to be no tangible reward along the way, allow God to be the exceeding great reward of your life's Journey (Genesis 15:1). Take Him at His word. He makes all things beautiful in its own time (Ecclesiastes 3:11). When you chose to remain faithful, sooner or later, you will find the eternal beauty in all that God allows you to encounter in life's Journey.

Prosperity Spree

We are living in a world where we're constantly bombarded with not just the cares of this life, but the desire to pursue more and more of the things of this life. We are all vulnerable to falling into the trap of this prosperity spree and should therefore seek to resist and avoid it. At this point we should have already come to the realization that worldly prosperity cannot fill our lives with joy or offer any meaningful form of fulfillment. In fact, its pursuit might become a deterrent.

Never-the-less, our financial difficulties, coupled with our insecurities, can easily distract our focus. This distraction is even sharpened when we become hypnotized by the worldly success of those around us. It's harder to appreciate our humble, challenging circumstances when our peers seem to be flourishing materially. However, if our main purpose for living becomes diverted towards gaining prosperity then, we have no doubt diverted from God's ideal purpose and Will for us. We would have diverted from journeying on the Narrow Road and have crossed over to the Broad Road.

It is God's desire that we all prosper and be in good health (3 John 1:2). This; however, was never meant to be our main goals in life. By God's design, temporal prosperity should merely accompany us as we aim to fulfill a greater purpose.

Our mission as followers of Christ is to seek first the kingdom of God and His righteousness. In doing this, God will grant us all that equips us to live the joyful and fulfilling life, and even more, when He deems fit (Matthew 6:33). We should never neglect His mission or make it secondary in our lives in order to become prosperous or to maintain prosperity.

The things of this world are to support our life and mission as we journey on this earth. They are vehicles. They are merely objects that form part of the means by which we might effectively fulfill God's Plan for our lives. Their attainment is not an end or in other words, the life goal. They're not our reason for living. They cannot be. God has a higher and nobler purpose for all of us.

It makes no sense to gain all that you want at the expense of what you really need. What you need is the reigning presence of God with you and in you, nourishing and directing your Path. More of Him and fulfilling His mission for your life should be the lifelong goal of your pursuit.

So then, why not make it your pursuit in life to labor primarily for the things that are eternal - the things that are more rewarding and can pass from this life to the next?

We must be careful not to be overcome by difficult financial situations and chase after the things of this world because this will no doubt interfere in our interests and availability to fulfill God's mission for our lives. When our desires are on heavenly things, assuredly they will be fulfilled. Therefore, delight yourself in the Lord and He will grant you the desires of your heart (Psalm 37:4).

When your mission is wholeheartedly, being about your Master's business, He will care for you. Our heavenly father who adorns the grass that is here today and withers tomorrow, will no doubt provide for His precious children who He loves so much that He sent His Only Begotten Son to die for (Matthew 6:30 & John 3:16). He has already done the ultimate. Nothing else is too hard for Him to do for you.

It is not always easy to accept these promises when faced with the reality of unpaid bills, helpless children to provide for and an empty refrigerator. Yet you must recognize at all times that God is the Great Provider of all of us who are in His care. In the presence of little He is no less the Great Provider as He is in the presence of abundance. Neither is He less faithful to those with little material wealth, as He is to His Children who have plenty.

He allows seasons of drought for you to appreciate the rainy season when it comes around. In the presence of the drought He will grant you blessings that you cannot attain during the seasons of plenty. His timing and reasoning are perfect.

During your seasons of drought, rather than focusing on your lack, focus on the love, presence, power and goodness of God and be constantly reminded that His ultimate Will for your life is worth far more than your suffering.

Never lose sight of the thought that God is willing to take you through whatever circumstances necessary to have His Will fulfilled in your life. There will be times when God's provisions are apparently inadequate and this inadequacy might very well be a reflection of the measure of faith that He intends to mold into you as you trust Him to fulfill your need. There are priceless virtues that He desires to impart to you, even through your times of need.

God values the great work that He wants to accomplish in your life. This He values even more than silver or gold. As you work to fulfill your material needs, take care not to allow this to interfere with God's eternal

Plan for you. God's Plan for you is more valuable than temporal treasures. Endeavor to trust His heart and His insight.

In the Greek myth, the poor King Midas who was eager for wealth was granted the opportunity to make one wish. His wish was *a golden touch*. Everything King Midas touched was turned to gold - the flowers in his garden, his food, his friends, his daughter - his entire palace. Instead of growing happier with gold, the king grew very sad. Consequently, he requested for the wish to be reversed. He realized that when he didn't have the riches of gold, he was already blessed with the riches that make life meaningful.

Suppose you had one wish, what would it be? Would you ask God for that genuine desire to be saturated with the riches that make like meaningful? He longs to fill your life with these.

Part 5

Life Lessons

**It is in truly living that we capture the real meaning,
purpose and value of life**

IF YOU'RE NOW AT that place where you sincerely believe that God has been
doing something wonderful in your heart and for your life, you might ask:
"How do I really walk daily along the Pathway in my life's Journey?" That's
exactly what we'll talk about in this chapter.

God has re-created you into a new person for you to live a new life in
accordance with His design. Reading, hearing and talking about the
Christian walk are good, but walking the Journey is by far more exalted
and rewarding. You reap the rewards of this Journey on the Narrow Road
by making the effort to get off your couch in life and practically live - live
in accordance with God's design for your life.

If you have allowed the Holy Spirit to come in and control your life,
then there is so much potential for great things in you right now; so
many opportunities for you to live this glorious life to its fullest. So, why
not ensure that you leap out of your comfort zone and truly experience
journeying with God.

Imagine your best friend returning home from a great trip and sharing
with you news of all the splendors of the trip. While you can share in the
pleasure of hearing about the trip, you cannot truly reap the rewards that
come with living the experience unless you personally take that trip. The
same goes for the Christian life.

Feasting on spiritual materials, such as in worship services, elevate our
thoughts and give us moments of highs. Through them our lives can be

empowered and we become equipped for growth. They strengthen us on our Journey – but they're not the actual Journey.

We must be reminded that these are only preparation and support for the real experience. Living the experience is what brings to life concrete rewards. Our Christian lives will be fruitless and unfulfilling if we do not allow God to flex our spiritual muscles. We must digest the written and spoken word and allow God to use them to nurture us to maturity in our everyday life.

Allow God to consistently mold you into that person of virtue so that you can live the life of virtue that He envisions for you. Only the virtuous person can live the virtuous life. In becoming a new person in Christ, God has been molding His joy into you. But *the joy of the Lord and fulfillment in life are unchained in you only as you abide in God and live in accordance with His Will.* This is how true joy and fulfillment is continuously experienced in the life of every follower of Christ.

Chapter 9

Claiming God's Presence & Power over Your Life

The Virtue of Excellence

GOD LOVES PERFECTION. HE created a perfect world, with perfect beings, in a perfect setting. By God's Standard, excellence peaks at perfection. Shouldn't we too cultivate this Standard? Well, this is exactly God's Standard for you.

Christ encourages that we should be perfect even as our Father in heaven (Matthew 5:48). We cannot attain this Standard on our own. It is attainable through empowerment from God. It is a godly principle to strive for perfection in every single aspect of our life. God's arms are outstretched to reach down to you and lift you to the height that He desires for you to ascend to.

When we have a genuine desire for God's Will to be accomplished in our lives, He will no doubt empower us to do so with excellence. This is demonstrated through King Solomon (1 Kings 3:3-15). When Solomon became king he saw the surmountable task of governing God's people. He poured out his heart to God. He related that he feels like such a child, not knowing the first step to take yet his task is so great. He asked the Lord for the understanding to discern good from evil so that he could be an effective leader for God's people.

Solomon didn't ask God for riches, long life or the life of his enemies. His heartfelt desire was not a selfish one. He desired empowerment for the purpose of doing an excellent job at the task that God has designed for him to perform. For this reason God granted Solomon understanding and wisdom, beyond what anyone before or after him possessed. God also granted him riches above that of all the other kings around. In addition, God promised Solomon long life on the condition that he remained faithful to Him.

Like Solomon do you too at times feel like just a child when it comes to seeking to live an upright life that honors God and His Will for you? If so, that's exactly the level of dependence that God is expecting from you. All that you need is a desire and willingness to serve God with excellence and He will enable you to lead that life of excellence.

Excellence is not limited to merely an act. It's not even just a habit. It's a character trait. It is a virtue. It is a virtue that is attainable by those who consciously take the time to have it cultivated into their being. When it is cultivated, acts and habits of excellence naturally flow from your life. This is the person that God is nurturing you into becoming.

In seeking to please God at all times and to represent Him at all cost, He gradually coaches you into the art of living a life of excellence. You will achieve excellence in the fruits of your labor; your conduct, mannerism, and attitude towards people and life; because most significantly, you would first be attaining excellence in your character development. Excellence by God's standard is not defined by material worth or temporal achievements – but by eternal outcome.

Whoever you are, endeavor to be your best through Christ. Whatever you do, endeavor to allow God's empowerment for you to do it to the best of your ability. In so doing, you would have glorified God in who you are and through the life that you live.

The Highest Praise

Worship is a central aspect of the lives of all created beings. It is the theme of the lives of the heavenly angels. The angels surrounding God's throne utter ceaselessly "Holy, holy, holy, Lord God Almighty..." (Revelation 4:8). This sounds like a boring thing to do all day and all night, doesn't it?

The joy of this degree of worship is unknown to those who hardly find the energy to spend just moments of a day to sing God's praise. But great joy is unleashed when we express our gratitude and reverence to God.

We praise God in diverse ways. We praise God in:

- worship exercises (singing, praying, reading & exaltation of the Scripture, etc)

- allowing Him to renew our character into His likeness
- the manner in which we choose to live life

As the coast redwood trees tower upward towards the sun, as if in salutation to its nourishing rays that falls on their leaves, so too should we live in reverence and adoration towards God – the Source of our being and existence. The angels in heaven praise God ceaselessly. They've never experienced the joy of being redeemed. They've never experienced the grace and forgiveness that we humans have experienced. Yet they devote their entire existence to giving God the highest praise.

We owe our entire existence to God. Without Him we would not be here (John 1:1-4; Acts 17:28). Had it not been for God, we wouldn't know the joys of life or have the hope of eternal life. God has already given us everything (Acts 17:24&25). He has freely given us life and all the real splendors of life.

God is not dependent on our praise, or anything we can offer Him. When we praise God, we're not doing Him a favor. We're giving Him the reverence that He deserves. We're expressing our gratefulness for His goodness, love, mercy, generosity, forgiveness and graciousness towards us.

When someone has given you an amazing gift you want to express sincere gratitude that is acceptable to that person. We must therefore allow God to lift us above sin and mediocrity. This is the only way that we can appropriately thank Him from a heart made pure and a life renewed. That's the only way we can offer praise that is acceptable to God.

Praising God through devotional exercises is an acceptable format of worship. However, this form of worship has its limits. Unlike the angels that surround God's throne, our task as humans involve more than repeating words of praise in God's presence. We go about other daily activities. But, those moments in between church services and personal devotional exercises are also crucial.

To praise God continuously would therefore mean to yield to Him by allowing Him to consistently mold you into the person that He desires for you to be and, automatically, in living a life of praise. In so doing, you would have glorified His *name* by reflecting His character. From the very beginning, God created man in His own image and likeness, because He desired for man to reflect who He is. *God's greatest delight is for you to reflect His glory.* There's no higher praise than this!

Paul encourages that in our eating and drinking and in *all* that we do, we should do it to the glory and honor of God (1 Corinthians 10:31). When we do this, like the angels in heaven we worship God ceaselessly, day and night.

On the contrary, when we compartmentalize our lives where our spirituality is only one aspect of our lives, and it's not immersed into work, family, career and other aspects of life, we make a terrible mistake. Our spirituality should encompass every aspect of who we are and the way that we live life. This is the only way that we can allow God to govern our entire lives.

From the moment you awake in the morning to the moment you return to bed at night, in everything that you think and do, seek to glorify God. You will be amazed at the remarkable difference this makes to your relationship with God and the quality of joy and fulfillment that you experience over every aspect of your life.

It is in being that person of excellence, in living the life of excellence, that we give God the highest praise. Therefore, offer yourself, holy and pleasing to God, as a living sacrifice – this is your true and proper worship (Romans 12:1).

A Living Sacrifice

God's Plan for your life will never just be only about satisfying you. You are being sanctified for an even greater purpose. Regardless of how unique your purpose in this life, it must ultimately be to the glory and honor of God. It must be for the good of others. The life of Christ exemplifies this perfectly.

God has done the ultimate towards saving mankind by sending Christ to die on the cross. He will continue to do all that is required to save individuals and to uplift each life on earth. As we have seen so far, saving humanity is big on God's agenda. He has included you in this huge Plan. He desires your input. As we accept His Calling He enlightens us in order to illuminate our lives for our benefit and also for us to be a beacon so that through us others can be called.

He has called you, to call others. He has saved you, to also save others. He has blessed you, to bless others. He wants to use you, so that He can in return use others. God's work in your life makes a dual statement. It voices His unending love for you. It also declares the high calling He has for your life, in serving humanity. God's calling for you, involves more than just the material or temporal things of this life and, has been designed to conclude with eternal outcomes and eternal rewards.

God's unique Plan for you may not be a single purpose. It may not be as clear-cut as say being a missionary to a foreign land. One thing for sure, He wants to use your entire being to speak to the hearts and minds of everyone that comes into contact with you. He wants to use your entire life.

He wants to communicate His presence, His love, joy, compassion and forgiveness through you. He wants you to be a channel through which these virtues flow into the lives of others. People, who are in contact with you, will experience your God. If faithful, they too will allow themselves to become a channel through which the revitalizing effect of experiencing the Essence of Life's Journey will flow to the hearts and lives of others.

Making yourself available to be controlled by God will mean allowing Him to influence the words you speak, the decisions you make, the deeds you perform. All will be done in accordance with His timing and in His manner.

In so doing, you are allowing the presence of God to abide with you continuously. Heaven will surround you on earth. You will become a bearer of light for the Light of the world; a mouthpiece for the Living Word; and a vessel of honor for the Bread of Life. You would have made yourself available for God to use you in whatever capacity He desires.

In choosing to offer your life as a living sacrifice onto the Lord, you must ensure that this sacrifice is acceptable to Him. Otherwise, your sacrifice would have been in vain. During Old Testament time when God's people made animal sacrifice, there was something that was necessary in order for this sacrifice to be acceptable to God. The animal must be spotless – without blemish (Leviticus 22:21).

We've all been tarnished by sin. Can an Ethiopian change his skin or a leper his spots (Jeremiah 13:23)? They can't change their traits but their Creator can. We can't make ourselves spiritually spotless, but God can. And when He does, this spotless being becomes the perfect sacrifice we can ever offer to Him.

If, unfortunately, you find yourself back in the mud, He can pick you up and give you another bath (1 John 1:9 & 2:1). He's a loving and forgiving God. We too should love Him enough to do what is necessary to allow Him to safeguard us from falling into the mud.

We have a responsibility to ensure that in presenting ourselves to God, we are continuously presenting to Him an acceptable sacrifice. Grateful children do not exploit their parents' generosity and goodwill towards them. Instead they reward it with the true obedience that delights their parents. Let us endeavor to preserve ourselves as an acceptable sacrifice for God's pleasure, for His glory and for His divine industry.

Safeguard the Avenues to Your Soul

We perceive the world through our senses: our sight, hearing, smelling, tasting and touching. The corresponding sense organs are the avenues to our soul. These are the windows through which external influences enter our being.

Through constant prayer and obedience, we allow God to safeguard our soul. While we depend on God to cleanse and purge our entire being from negativity, we must also allow Him to safeguard these avenues to our soul. We have a responsibility to remain pure. We have a responsibility over what we allow to enter our heart, mind and body.

It is important to thoughtfully monitor the things you allow to enter your system through – your choice of entertainment, the TV programs you watch, the things you listen to, your diet, etc. These can either build or destroy the quality of person God is molding you into and the quality of life He has prepared for you to live. Choose wisely. Whatever you allow to enter through the avenues of your soul will greatly influence how readily you will accommodate God's presence in your life and your availability to be used by Him.

By appealing to Eve's senses, the devil convinced her to disobey God (Genesis 3:1-6). He first fed convincing words of lies to her. Next, when Eve looked at the tree of the knowledge of good and evil, she found it to be *pleasant to the eyes*. These combined were enough to communicate all the persuasion necessary to sway her mind from God's truth.

Eve knew God's Will. She understood His command. But knowing wasn't enough. She started to defile herself from the very moment that she gave attention to the enticing words of the devil. In opening the windows of her soul for the devil to come in, she automatically closed the door to God's influence on her heart and mind.

On the other hand, Daniel and the three Hebrew boys understood the significance of guarding the avenues to their souls (Daniel 1). As a result, they stood head and shoulders above their Babylonian peers. When presented with the opportunity to eat from the menu of the King of Babylon, Daniel firmly maintained that he will not *defile himself* with the king's food and wine. Instead they continued with the simple diet that God impressed on their hearts. In adhering to this decision, God was glorified. In the end the four men were more radiant in outward appearance and 10 times wiser than the king's wise men who fed from the king's diet.

If we allow God, He will mold our desires towards genuinely appreciating purity and godliness. In return, we should make the effort to feast on the things that are spiritually uplifting and obediently avoid those that destroy us in any way. Your body is God's dwelling place (1 Corinthians 6:19). It is sacred and should be treated accordingly.

Paul admonishes that whatever things are true, honest, just, pure, lovely, of good report, virtuous and praise worthy – think on them (Philippians 4:8). These we should feed our minds on. These we should allow to permeate the very atmosphere that we breathe.

Your Inner Circle

We do not exist within a vacuum. There will never be an isolated human actor at any given time in the stage of life here on earth. God designed for you to interact with others for reasons He knows best. It is therefore important to grasp exactly how people were designed to fit into God's Plan for your life and you fit into theirs. You must be mindful of the influence you have on the lives of others, and how they are allowed to influence your own life.

If your life is lived according to the directives of God, that means He brought to your life every single person that is present in your life for a special reason. That includes: the good, the bad and the seemingly indifferent persons. Never exclude anyone from sharing into your life.

Regardless of how simple or unseen, the presence of even irritable persons in our lives means something to God. We need to therefore allow God to determine the place each person should occupy in our lives. That's it - there is a place in your life for all the people in your life.

The problem we usually have is: where do they fit? For example, we might give our family far too little room and priority in our lives and so these precious relationships may suffer. On the contrary there might be hurtful people that we haven't taken the liberty to guard from permeating our soul through their influence in our inner-circle.

In your unique relationships, as God deems fit, it is important to let Him:

1. Control the influences in your inner-circle
2. Firmly position you, and/or
3. Empower you with resistance from damaging influences

Let God Control Your Inner-circle

If we embrace into the bosom of our lives, influences that conflict with God's influence, then it may become very difficult and even impossible for us to glorify God through our lives.

By surrounding yourself with close friends who are faithless, negative, gossiping and backbiting; who rip down God's principles with their words and deeds, you will eventually suffer the impact of their aura. As you inhale their miasma, sooner or later you too will, internally process then, exhale a similar concussion. These people may not hurt you intentionally or directly, but you will become damaged through habitual close association with them.

Pray over your inner-circle and allow God to control it. It might become necessary for Him to weed out people who pull you down and barricade His Plans for your life. This does not equate to breaking contacts and interactions. What it implies is exerting control over their inappropriate influence in your life. This may be a re-positioning of their role in your life. Like for example, a re-positioning from being a friend who calls you up for daily gossip to becoming a friend who shares in your Bible study group. In re-positioning the destructive people in your inner circle, your soul would have been safeguarded and preserved to be used for God's sacred purpose.

In the passing moment, you may not realize the impact of others on your life. However, from retrospection, years later their impact on your decisions, way of thinking or habits formed will be easily detected – sometimes after it's already too late.

It is not a single smoking episode that results in the development of lung disease in a chain smoker; rather it is the habitual exposure. Accordingly, you do not need to be a chain-smoker to suffer the impact of chain-smoking. Close habitual association with a chain-smoker, while he smokes, is enough to place you at as close a risk or an even closer risk to lung-disease than the smoker himself. The same effort that is practically necessary to guard our physical health is also needed to safeguard the other aspects of our being such as our morality or spirituality.

A casual contact with an ungodly person may not impact our outlook on life as in having that person as a bosom friend. As smoke to the lungs so do words and actions travel to our psyche and either elevate or mar our values, thoughts and attitude.

Exerting control over your inner-circle may become the dividing line between:

- who you are/who you are becoming – and – who God intends for you to be
- where you are now/where you are heading – and – where God intends for you to be

The nature of your traveling companions in life's Journey speaks of who you are and the direction of your destination. If I know I'm really destined to head north, I can't just hop on the bus with my friend who is going south, and still expect to reach north. Life just doesn't work that way. That would defeat the whole purpose of my journey. This is a point we must practically consider for our lives' Journey.

Let God Firmly Position You

When essential issues such as morality conflicts with your inner-circle relationships, then let it not be that you compromise godly morals in an effort to keep a close association. Otherwise, your Journey will be hindered. Neither is it possible for you to head in the same direction in the presence of such conflict. Can 2 walk together if they don't agree (Amos 3:3)? In the end, somebody or both persons will end up compromising their morals in order to journey together in life.

Oil and water cannot mix together to form a true solution. When added to each other, they automatically separate because their components are different; the oil will float above the water. There are unique forces that bind oil together differently from the forces that bind water together. These forces keep the two substances apart while binding them to molecules like themselves. The unique composition of oil and water would have to be altered in order for them to be thoroughly mixed into a true solution. The same applies to believers and unbelievers.

It is crucial to be aligned with people whose life goals are consistent with the principles that God has impressed on your heart. If your goals and desires are ordered according to God's Plan and their principles strikingly contrast with those of persons in your inner circle, either of 2 things might need to happen in order for God to accomplish them through you:

1. Your bosom friends change their lives according to God's ideal and you all journey together
2. You make the decision to progress by God's design and allow Him to position you within the inner circle He sees fit

Otherwise, you might resort to a third option where: you remain stationary with those friends or move at the same pace and/or spiritual direction influenced by the pulling effect of the relationship. Every close relationship we form will, directly or indirectly, either push us towards or pull us away from God's ideal for our lives.

We can encourage people to make godly decisions but in the end, the choice is left up to them. We cannot drag them along on the Narrow Road. We cannot afford to divert God's direction and rich blessings for our Journey for this cause either.

Lot had a similar experience with his dear wife. She looked back at what she was leaving behind after God commanded them to flee Sodom and Gomorrah because of the impending destruction (Genesis 19:1-29). She chose not to leave behind the life in that city. When Lot's wife re-considered leaving, he had to make a decision as to whether he will continue to move forward by God's design or share her fate in being destroyed with the city. Lot didn't abandon his wife. In making the decision to obediently move ahead as directed by God, while his wife decided to remain behind, the two automatically moved apart.

The decision to move forward spiritually is one that we're all confronted with at some point in our lives. Our positive response may result in a repositioning of persons in our inner circle. Will we choose God's ideal for us? Or will we choose to share the fate of those who refuse to walk with us towards God's ideal? This will be determined by whether we allow those in our inner circle to push us towards or pull us away from glorifying God through our lives.

Allow God to position your life at the altitude He desires for it to be, regardless of the consequences that follow. It will require great boldness, but choose God's ideal for you. In journeying ahead, you may very well become a predecessor to some of those who you would have otherwise lagged behind with.

Let God Empower You with Resistance

There is no one-cap-fit-all approach to life. As humans we're all eager for that recipe for living the good life but, not every approach will apply to every individual and every situation we face in this life. That is exactly why it is so very important for us to hear from God - stay connected to Him. We must be keen in listening to His voice as He seeks to communicate to us and direct us through the varied, unique issues we'll face in life.

As is evident, not everyone who you encounter will choose to share in the Journey with you on the Narrow Road. But, some of these people are in the category of loved ones. Others you might have even made some form of obligations to, prior to commencing this Journey.

How then do you move forward? Simply make that decision to move forward and God will direct you accordingly.

We cannot just pitch people out of our lives. Christ chose 12 disciples, none were angels and one was the devil's advocate. Christ never turned back anyone from following him. But, the rich presence of his Father strengthened and safeguarded him from the negative influence of those who remained close to him. When God has allowed negative people to remain in our lives, we must allow Him to empower us to withstand their negative effect on accomplishing His Will for our lives.

As we journey, we should prayerfully consult the Lord concerning safeguarding our souls, while being a good friend or close companion to those who need us. When we make it a duty to selfishly shut out obnoxious people from our lives for the purpose of moving forward, we may very well defeat God's purpose. We may very well prevent God from using their rough edges to refine our rough edges as a means of perfecting us. We may also close a door through which God desires to minister to a helpless soul. Those are some of the very people who followed Christ and who he ministered to daily while on earth.

We must be willing to exercise patience towards others and trust God's reason for allowing them into our lives. We are not living in an ideal world with ideal people or ideal situations. We will as a result have to endure undesirable encounters with undesirable personalities at times.

The important lesson here is to have God safeguard our souls, with the intention of avoiding negative influences and deterrents the Enemy will place in our way in the form of people, as a stumbling block. The answer is not in ignoring the obnoxious, hating the seemingly unlovable and turning your back on the undesirable.

The answer is in not allowing their close affiliation with you to rob you of experiencing God's guiding presence, His blessings and therefore preventing you from living in accordance with God's Will for your life. The answer is in developing and maintaining an intimate relationship with God and seeking to discern His Will over your daily life - even in your relationship with others.

Your Aura

If you observe a large city, there is usually much noise and confusion; while a large garden is often serene and peaceful. A person with bad mannerism is repulsive and evokes negative feelings in the atmosphere around him. The objects, people and activities in the environment all contribute to its atmosphere. We all have our personal atmosphere. It is outwardly influenced by our expressions, the manner in which we conduct ourselves and relate to others.

What is the atmosphere surrounding your presence? Does it perfume the air others have to breathe when they're around you?

Christ attracted others to himself because the atmosphere around him brought praise to God, and life and hope to those in his presence. It is important to strive to maintain an internal and external atmosphere that nurtures positive thoughts and attitude. With its many burdens and woe, this world by itself is often a frustrating place to be. Often people gravitate towards that place where they can find contentment, peace and refuge. Or they gravitate towards that person in whom these virtues are present.

On the other hand, just like there were those who found the company of Christ a reproach, the same will apply to the company of His followers.

Those who made a conscious decision not to follow Christ were offended and threatened by his presence. They feared the consequences of his influence and for that reason they failed to enjoy the precious aura that surrounded him.

Not everyone will enjoy your company. When your life is in tune with the divine Will of God, you cannot take blame for this predicament. You should never compromise godly principles to gain the friendship or favor of those who take offense to true godliness.

Let it be that in loving you, others would have come to love your Savior; in hating you, they would have hated your Savior, because you would have represented your Savior to them in who you are and your attitude towards them.

When Christ becomes the reason for your existence, then whatever you do or say will be done to glorify God and not yourself. You will not find much interest or virtue in defending yourself for the sake of boosting your self-image or reputation. You will firmly refuse to compromise godly principles. Such freedom you would have found in Christ in living this life of joy and fulfillment.

Pleasing God will therefore become more important to you than pleasing yourself or satisfying other people's perception of you. This is the place God wants you to be. When you allow this, then the aura around you will be a genuinely godly one. Not one that is created merely out of an attempt to exalt self; but one that flows from within, out of a true desire to glorify God according to the person He is fashioning you to be.

The follower of Christ is often the first point of contact between the unbeliever and Christ. Most unbelievers will first come to Christ, through contact with a follower of Christ. God designed it that way. The invisible God designed for His Children to visibly represent Him to the world. Your aura can either push others from or pull them towards basking in the presence of your Lord and feasting on the Essence of Life's Journey.

For those who have not established a personal walk with God, your presence should be such that by being around you they sense the joyful, gentle, peaceful aura of Christ. Your presence should be like a breath of fresh air to those who are intoxicated with the misery of this life. Your expressions, words and mannerisms speak of your connection with your Savior.

Speak Life

The impact of the written and spoken word can hardly be erased after they have been read or listened to. It is so important that we choose to speak carefully. Many lives and reputations have been painfully marred by the appalling influence of gossip, lies and destructive criticisms. The insidious danger of gossip is that it rarely looks offensive unless you are the victim or closely related to the victim. Sadly though, only the insecure and spiritually weak find pleasure in tearing down others.

A helpful cliché I've heard my sister used is: "never speak ill of the dead or someone who has turned their back". People should be around to defend themselves if we utter anything ill against them. Let it be part of your character trait and a habit of yours to be your brother's keeper. If someone errs, then speaking this outside of his presence is a selfish endeavor and an unwise attempt to initiate positive change. Speak purposively to preserve and protect the good image of others, in both their presence and absence.

Seek to act based on the goodwill of others even in the very words used over their lives. When through God you come to experience the Essence of Life you speak life, and not hatred or death, over the lives of others. If the omniscient God has dealt with you so kindly in preserving you, despite your glitches and blunders, shouldn't you likewise act in the best interest of others who are mistake prone, just as you are? God has given us life through the Living Word. Likewise, we should seek to impart life to others through our words.

Hurtful words can damage a person's feelings, self-image and life. I once heard a man said that, as a child, his mother repeatedly told him that he is just as worthless as his father; that he would never amount to anything good - and she was right. This became a self-fulfilling prophesy in his life. He believed the words of his mother to the extent that he brought life to those words and never saw it possible to break free from them throughout his entire life.

What words do you choose to decorate the atmosphere around you? Death and life are in the power of the tongue (Proverbs 18:21). Choose to speak life. Choose to speak life and not death into your life and into the life of others.

Yet, what comes out of the mouth, is originally a derivative of the heart (Matthew 15:18). The best method for cleaning up our mouth is therefore to first allow God to clean up our heart. This will in return, renovate our entire aura.

Chapter 10

Claiming Godly Virtues

Unity with Your Fellowmen

WORLD WAR II IS noted as the most devastating war in the history of the world. Following this war was the signing of peace treaties as official statements to ensure that the world would be at peace and not experience a similar devastating conflict.

The treaties were successful in laying down the physical ammunitions but, unfortunately, not the ammunitions of the heart. For about another 44 years, conflicts and tensions remained between the opposing alliances of World War II. The end of World War II gave rise to, not peace and unity, but the Cold War. Nations were still at enmity in their hearts.

Time after time, so many arguments and proposals have been presented for world peace and unity. Can the nations of the world be one with each other? Can men truly be at peace with each other?

Being at peace with each other, starts with being at peace with God. Anything in our hearts that work as a barrier between us and God will also place us at enmity with each other. Hatred, greed, malice, pride, prejudice and any sin in our heart will form a barrier between us being at peace with God, and will also hinder our relationship with our fellowmen. To be at peace with God and consequently our fellowmen, our hearts and lives must first be renewed and united with God.

Like joy, peace is a quality of God (Galatians 5:22&23). The new life in Christ comes with renewed relationship with both God and the children of God. Spiritual oneness with fellow believers is not limited to joining a particular church and calling each other brothers and sisters. True brotherhood comes from something deeper. This transcends national, religious, denominational, racial, and cultural boundaries. It is rooted in the very Spirit of God. It is rooted in sharing into the experience of the very Essence of Life's Journey.

When Jesus was on earth, his prayer was that we would be made one with him and our Father in the same way that he is one with the Father. Also, that we will be one with each other, just as he is one with the Father. Before Christ left this earth, his promise to his disciples was the presence of him and his Father with them through the Holy Spirit.

Remember how the Holy Spirit makes us one with God and empowers us to live the joyful and fulfilling life? It is this same Spirit that made Christ one with the Father; it is also the very same Spirit that makes us untied with each other (John 17:20-23). The Holy Spirit imparts godly qualities of brotherly love and peace into our hearts. The Holy Spirit is within each believer as an invisible, unbroken chain that binds us together. This is the basis on which men can be completely united with each other.

The Holy Spirit is the binder between us and God and us and each other (John 14:16-20). All who share oneness with God will also experience oneness with each other. This oneness will occur irrespective of the pervasive boundaries on this earth that separate people in their hearts and motives. The Spirit of God displaces and transcends all of these boundaries. Love, peace and unity among men and nations can only be found when hearts have been knitted together, in Christ.

As your oneness with Christ comes with oneness in purpose, purity of heart and goodwill towards each other, the same applies to oneness with your fellowmen. You would share similar overall goals and vision with each other. You won't need to fight war to make peace. You will not need to sign peace treaties to prevent wars. What you would truly need is to become one in Christ - and you would have attained that.

Those who have found unity in Christ will no doubt find unity among themselves, in the presence of dissention on earth. Those who experience the peace of Christ will find peace among each other, despite worldwide wars and turmoil. Unity with our fellowmen is a remarkable blessing that God desires to enrich our new life.

What a delight when we find genuine spiritual brotherhood with our fellowmen. We can sincerely say "my brother" without doing so out of mere formality or make-believe. Spiritual brotherhood is even deeper and richer than biological brotherhood. When biological brothers may be at enmity with each other and do not share the same Spirit, purpose and Narrow Road in this life, spiritual brothers enjoy these blessings.

Spiritual brothers share together in the Essence of Life's Journey - they share what matters the most in this life. They experience rejuvenating fellowship with each other. This was Christ's prayer and promise for your renewed life. God desires that all His spiritual children share in this level of brotherhood. His Spirit in you empowers you to do so with others who are likewise empowered.

As the psalmist declares:

> *"1 How good and pleasant it is*
> *when God's people live together in unity!*
>
> *2 It is like precious oil poured on the head,*
> *running down on the beard,*
> *running down on Aaron's beard,*
> *down on the collar of his robe.*
> *3 It is as if the dew of Hermon*
> *were falling on Mount Zion.*
> *For there the* LORD BESTOWS HIS BLESSING,
> *even life forevermore. "* (Psalm 133)

You will not always be able to have peaceful, cohesive relationships with everyone, especially those who live contrary to godly principles. At the same time, as much as is possible, strive to be at peace with *everyone* (Romans 12:18).

The Blessings of Turning the Other Cheek

Turning the other cheek, going the extra mile and giving both the cloak and the coat (Matthew 5:38-41), can be very difficult in a world that deems humility as a sign of weakness. Unwillingness to fight back automatically sends just the right message to boost the ego of attackers and often propels them to exert even greater threat and attack.

In a world that nurtures arrogance, exercising humility may at times cause us to feel weak and foolish. But if it is weak and foolish to exercise humility, Christ would have been the biggest fool and weakling. He died for those who killed him. Yet he wasn't a fool or a weakling. He possessed virtues that surpassed human reasoning. Humility is a sign of spiritual maturity.

It takes humility to exercise mercy and forgiveness or, in other words, turn the other cheek.

It was William Shakespeare who penned these words in his well-known comedy *The Merchant of Venice* (paraphrased):

> *"Mercy drops from heaven on the place beneath*
> *It is a double blessing*
> *It blesses him that gives and him that receives*
> *It is a finer thing to a king than his crown itself*
> *Because it's a quality of God Himself*
> *Earthly power comes nearest to God's when justice is mingled with mercy"*

Indeed, mercy and forgiveness convey blessings that flow to both the giver and the intended recipient. Exercising mercy and forgiveness is a liberating experience. Likewise, not only the recipient, but also the giver, is withheld from such blessings when he refuses to forgive and exercise mercy. The Holy Spirit cannot thrive in an unmerciful, unforgiving and revengeful heart. Automatically, in nurturing such a heart, we rob ourselves of enjoying the best of this life.

Most significantly, mercy and forgiveness are qualities of God; so as fallen humans, being able to exercise them selflessly, speaks of the person you have become in Christ. It demonstrates that you have surrendered to your Lord and that He has renewed your heart.

It requires strength of character to turn the other cheek. Turning the other cheek means being able to exercise mercy and to forgive someone who has deliberately inflicted hurt on you. It means to refrain from retaliating to evil with evil. It means going as far as to even allow the attacker the opportunity to hurt you all over again, if necessary.

This is a very difficult concept to embrace. There's no doubt about that. However, it's a godly one. Solomon advises: "Let not truth and mercy leave you: bind them around your neck, write them in your heart. In so doing you will find favor and good understanding in the sight of God and man" (Proverbs 3:3&4).

It is interesting to bear in mind that just as others have inflicted hurt on your life, you too have inflicted hurt on the lives of others, in words and deeds, consciously and unconsciously. Wouldn't you want to be forgiven? Christ admonishes us to do to others as we would have them do to us (Matthew 7:12). This includes the mercy and forgiveness we would like to have manifested towards us, had we been in the position of the offender.

It takes genuine love to exercise mercy and forgiveness. We must first be at that place where, as God commands, we love others as we love ourselves. Love is a fundamental principle of being able to turn the other cheek.

Therefore, choose to love, even when the reality exist that your love might be misused. Choose to give, even when it's obvious that your gifts might be exploited. Choose to repay evil with good, even when this might be slighted. These are qualities of God and; therefore, are godly principles to live by. In fact, these are God's expectations for your new life. He's willing to empower you to live at this altitude and even beyond. Are you willing to do so?

When you have come to love others, as God loves, then turning the other cheek becomes easier and more logical.

Love as God Loves

To love as God loves goes beyond showing love to others and playing the role of a loving person. Quite often we know how to show love but we don't truly know how to love. Circumstances; however, usually reveal the difference between the mere show and the real thing. When we truly love, whether or not we make an effort for it to show, one way or another, it will show. Wouldn't it therefore be better to truly love?

To love as God loves, means to actually love. It means to love unconditionally. It means to love perfectly. To love perfectly is not a quality of mere fallen humans - it is divine.

God is love (1 John 4:8). Like joy, love cannot be reproduced or regenerated. Love is derived only from God. It is a quality of God. More so, love embodies who God is. We love unconditionally only when we have the Spirit of God dwelling within us, controlling us. That Spirit of love empowers us to love. This is how God, and only God, enables us to love unconditionally as He loves.

Christ commands that we love unconditionally, perfectly, even as God loves (Matthew 5: 43-48). Love is such a significant aspect of the nature of God, that it is a significant identifying mark of those who are His children. God's people will love as God loves because they have attained this from God. This quality tags us as God's. In loving others as Christ did, we are automatically identified as his followers (John 13:34&35). This love declares that such a person is in personal contact with and has surrendered to the Source of love.

Love is not just an emotion. It is a principle that governs our feelings, attitude and goodwill towards others. It is the genuine care and concern we should have in our hearts for everyone - including those who do not love us in return; including even those who hurt us in return.

Of all the virtues and the gifts that God can bestow in your life, the greatest is love. The apostle Paul speaks eloquently on this matter. Without love - we are *nothing*. We could be blessed with prophesying, linguistic skills, the languages of angels, faith that moves mountain, great knowledge and understanding of deep mysteries, yet it is all empty when we do not love unconditionally. We may give to the poor and even be willing to die for a godly cause, but without this love, even these profit us nothing. (1 Corinthians 13:1-3)

Love is persevering and kind. Love is not envious, boastful, conceited, selfish or easily angered. It does not produce evil thoughts or wrong behavior. It does not rejoice in evil but rejoices in the truth. Love is eternal - it never ends; it never fails. (1 Corinthians 13:4-7)

We love God because He first loved us (1John 4:19). While we were sinners, enemies of God, He loved us and sent His Son to die for our redemption (Romans 5:5-10). We too must come to love our enemies first, while they are our enemies. We must love even the seeming un-loveable. This is the genuine love that comes only from God. When your enemies experience this love that they do not deserve, it may speak virtue into their hearts and action towards you - and even towards God.

A rich lawyer questioned Christ about how he can gain eternal life (Luke 10:25-28). Christ's reply was that obtaining eternal life is summed up in one great principle: ultimate love for God and loving others as ourselves. This is eternal life. We should love others as much as we love ourselves.

This includes our enemies. We should desire the very best for them, as we would ourselves.

Have nothing in your heart towards another person, except for love; in loving others you would have fulfilled God's commandants (Romans 13:8-10). Thou shall not murder, steal, commit adultery, bear false witness and covet - simply means *you must love others as yourself.* Thou shall have no other gods, thou shall have no physical representation of God, thou shall not misuse God's name and thou shall keep the Sabbath holy - simply means *you must love God with all your heart, soul, mind and strength.* Love fulfils the law because it doesn't hurt others; it doesn't offend God either.

We cannot truly love God unless we love those around us (1 John 4:20). People are God's beloved. People are special. We all get to walk this earth only once. Each person is irreplaceable, which attest to the true value of each one of us. People are more than their behavior and attitude. It's so important that we make use of every opportunity we have to treat the people God has placed in our lives, just as special as they truly are.

Three things will last to the end - faith, hope and love; but the greatest of them all, is love (1 Corinthians 13:13). This is because all the qualities of God are wrapped up in love. Faith, hope, peace, joy, forgiveness and all the attributes that flow from God to us are bound by love. Love governs all the blessings that God is bestowing on your life. The same will govern your correct thoughts, motives and attitude towards others too.

Pray that God will fill you with the unconditional love that our world needs so desperately. This is an essential ingredient in your life's Journey. It's an essential ingredient in fulfilling God's mission for your life and to be set free to enter into and abide in His joy.

The love of God flows into your heart when you surrender to the Holy Spirit's influence in your life (Romans 5:5). In experiencing the fullness of God's recreating, redirecting and replenishing power in your life, you become filled with godly qualities that are needed for you to be your very best and to live life at its very peak. Why not allow the Lord to thoroughly recreate in you that beautiful heart of unconditional love.

Serving Humanity as Christ Served

There is no profession, no task, more noble, dignified and exalted as the task that God has called each individual to do in serving humanity, regardless of what nature of service that may be. God's tasks for you may include a salaried job, family duties and/or ministerial or voluntary services.

Regardless of where you serve, it's never just about where you are positioned, but who positioned you. It's not about the nature of the tasks you perform but who assigned you this task and for what purpose. When God is in charge of our lives then we should value where He places us and what He desires to be fulfilled through us, even if we do not fully understand this mission.

Typically, we are cultured to believe that only selected professions and selected tasks in society are noble. For that reason we covet these, whether at home, in the workplace, at church or in the community. In so doing, we also neglect other tasks because they're not readily admired. But, *what makes a task dignified is not the magnitude of the task itself: it is 'the manner in which it is performed' and 'the value of its impact'*. Both of which can hardly be determined superficially.

In washing his disciples' feet, Christ taught them humility. In sweeping the floor, we make a difference to the atmosphere enjoyed by those present. Helping an elderly or disabled person across the street makes a difference in how that person gets across and the warmth transmitted to that heart. These are all simple tasks that do have profound impacts.

The impact of your labor may go unnoticed or be undermined by others, but to God be the glory - He sees far deeper than man sees. He is glorified when His Will is done in our lives, even when nobody acknowledges it. Let's look for example at Jeremiah, who was ordained and equipped by God to be a prophet (Jeremiah 1:1-10). He was given the task of calling back to God the rebellious nation of Judah that was heading for destruction.

Jeremiah's great work was overlooked by these, his own people. Instead of being rewarded, he was mocked, hated, rejected, falsely accused and imprisoned (Jeremiah 12:6; 18:18; 37:11-17). But this in no wise marred the reality that his was a job well-done. When overwhelmed by this reproach from everyone, he became discouraged from continuing God's work. But his inspiration to fulfill God's Will was far greater than his discouragement.

When he refrained from preaching God's word, in his heart it became like fire shut up in his bones (Jeremiah 20: 7-9). Living contrary to God's Will for His life was more painful for him to endure, than was the reproach he encountered from doing God's Will. His delight was in pleasing God.

It's always a pleasure when we receive approval and reward for our deeds. However, people's approval and rewards do not determine the real value of our deeds. *Our motives and attitude often validate the manner in which the task is performed and the, visible and invisible, worth of the deed.* For this reason, we do not have to be concerned that our task is below our skills and capability either. The right motives and attitude can transform the simplest of task into a glorious deed.

If the capacity in which you are positioned is exactly where God desires for you to be, then it's the best place for you to be until He desires to relocate you. If the task you have chosen is one which God desires for you to perform, then it is the noblest one for you. Execute it with great pride and dignity as if those who you serve are the Host and inhabitants of heaven. Believe it or not, indirectly, you are serving the Host of heaven. Aptly, in serving others, regardless of the capacity, we serve God. Ask God to show you ways in which you can serve Him through serving others. Keep your eyes open.

Be a Bridge Builder

It's important that we allow God to use us to initiate positive change. Allow Him to use you to instigate the difference that need to arise in your home, your church or your community, or anywhere for that matter.

This difference begins by allowing God to make you into a better person; that new person He desires for you to be. You will be amazed to know the level of impact a positive change in you can bring about in those around you. It starts with one person. Every great idea, every remarkable change was born through individuals.

Metaphorically, a bridge builder is someone who creates change that mobilizes people's lives. Bridge builders create change that enables people to cross over obstacles in life's journey. They help to build a connection from where people are to where they ought to be.

God is the chief bridge builder. He provided a way through Christ, through which we can all pass from sin to righteousness, death to life and earth to heaven. That lady, who helped her next-door neighbor with the bills after the sole bread-winner lost his job, became their bridge builder.

Will you be God's bridge builder for someone today?

In every facet of this life, people need bridges - Bridges to cross over their sufferings, addictions, imperfections and hopelessness. It's so very easy to see people's faults yet difficult to see their needs. But often the people who appear to live the most sinful lives or have the worst attitude are the ones who need the most help. They need bridges to cross over from being the person they are to becoming the person they should be.

Next time you have a bad encounter with someone, instead of just analyzing the persons fault, try to analyze that person's need. Try to analyze the structure of the bridge needed for that person to cross over. Find out how God might desire to use you to initiate a change in that person's life. You may very well be the bridge that God is building to help them cross over to the other side.

Making a change in your environment and in the life of others begins with initiating that change in you. It starts with you. That change in you will produce the change many persons need to mobilize their lives. Christ's followers are bridge builders. They're instigators of positive change. They are molded and shaped that way.

What influence do you have on the lives of those around you? What influence do you believe God desires for you to have? Why not ensure that you become that change that God intends for you to be.

The Living Word

As servants of God it is so important for us to see the big picture because religious people can easily become very self-centered when all focus and energy becomes divested into improving self. The things I eat, the way I dress, the places I go, developing my character, being happy, securing my reputation, ... Me, me, me can easily become the whole theme of our lives.

Nothing is wrong with taking care of ourselves and having our personal welfare at heart. However, when this absorbs our entire life then we obviously have gone off-track. We were saved to serve. A life that is occupied with only personal well-being forfeits this plan. God empowers us so that we can live abundantly and empower others to also live likewise.

Our life's mission is more than just our own needs and desires - whether spiritual or temporal. It's important to also acknowledge the needs of those around us. Our compassionate Savior lived among the people and walked among them daily. He did not serve from a distance where he was not acquainted with and touched by the feelings and needs of those around him.

To be able to have compassion on the suffering and needs of others, just like Christ did, we must allow the Lord to dispel some boundaries in our lives. Self-centeredness, prejudices, enmity, pride and vindictiveness must be removed from our hearts. God has to give us new eyes, heart and mind.

In the story of the Good Samaritan (Luke 10:25-37) which character more sums up your heart and attitude towards others? The priest and the Levite, who professed to be men of God, had not the love of God in their hearts to minister to a needy person that is outside of their faith. Yet a passerby, who seemed to be so insignificant that he wasn't even identified by a title, manifested the love of God towards the helpless dying stranger. He wasn't even one of the professed *holy* people.

This goes to show how much we too can become overly absorbed in fulfilling our religious obligations within our churches and in receiving our blessings, while still neglecting the work of God. When this happens, who do we pass on our way? Do you even see them?

The priest and Levite who passed the man by the wayside are hardly any worse than our attitude towards others if we neglect their physical and especially spiritual needs in our journey of a ritualistic and self-seeking religion. Such religion does not serve others and astoundingly, it does not serve God either. We cannot truly serve God until we learn to serve those who He loves dearly.

The Word of God comes to life in us, when we apply its principles to our lives. This is a significant means through which God will effectively reach others through our lives. There are real people in this world with real problems and real needs. The greatest sermons ever preached may never effectively minister to some lives unless they receive an intimate, personal contact with someone who possesses the love of God.

Christ recognized this when he offered to dine at the tax collector's house in the presence of other unbelievers (Mark 2:13-17). Christ saw the entire man and he ministered to the entire man - from the spiritual and physical to the social and emotional. Christ's first miracle was turning water into wine after the wine ran out at a wedding (John 2:1-11). He is concerned about our overall being.

Christ was indeed the Living Word. It is so important for us to share this Living Word with people. There is a place for sermonizing, theorizing and theologizing; but a religion embodied with only these is nothing more than a dead religion. There must also be a place for a practical religion that goes beyond the spoken and written word, and comes to life; comes into direct contact with not just the intellect but the very lives of people.

When we love people, it bothers us to see them live an overall poor quality of life. We won't only want to share a Bible study with them and invite them to church, while ignoring their hunger and nakedness. The genuine desire that leads us to minister to them will lead us to share God's truth with them verbally and will also inspire us to minister to their other needs as best as God enables us.

More hearts would have been changed and more lives renewed if like Christ, we covenant with God to seek out the lost, the broken-hearted, the poor and the outcasts and practically add life to their living. It is not hard to find people who need our help and support. They are everywhere - in every country, every city and every facet of life.

Let us pray that God anoints our eyes with spiritual eye-salve for us to see the needs of those around us; anoints our hearts to have compassion on them; anoints our minds to discern how to tend to their needs; and our hands, feet and lips to minister to them.

It is a self-centered life that often leads to misery. Not much joy and contentment can be experienced in a life that is geared towards serving and gratifying self. Instead, we must serve others, expecting nothing in return: do good things to those in need and not intentionally to those who can return the favor, or even openly, so that we can be deemed honorable.

We may never directly see the blessings of serving others. In fact, some of the very people we do good to will do us harm, but Christ advises us that we should do it anyway from a heart inspired by love (Matthew 5: 43-48). We should serve from a heart of love for God and humanity.

Give Freely to God

It is true that a seed must first be sown in order to reap a harvest. Accordingly, the seeds you sow may in return reflect the bounty of the harvest you reap. But does this mean that your giving to God should be influenced by what you want to get from Him in return? Not at all.

God has bestowed on us the glorious blessing of being filled with His Life-giving presence. He has made available to us the awesome privilege of having our lives enriched beyond measure with all that is required to live life abundantly. When God sent His Son to die for us, He did it out of unconditional love for us. He did it entirely for our welfare. When He blesses us, He also does it because of His goodness towards us. God is not a selfish giver. Neither does He encourage selfish giving. He wants us to give from a selfless heart.

While we will no doubt reap the rewards of giving, this should not become our motive for giving. Rather than selfish motives we should be driven by love for God and others. Otherwise, when we say we give, we don't truly give. What we do in reality is make an investment for ourselves. We would be selfishly investing our tithe, offerings, time and talent, for the sake of benefitting from the returns. But such self-seeking venture certainly displeases God who has freely given all to us.

God has gifted to us all that, through legitimate means, we possess:

- our selves / our lives
- our assets:
  - time
  - talent
  - treasure

In return, we should give God of our all. We should give Him from all of our substance.

It is often an easier decision to share a bit of our assets than it is to surrender ourselves to God. With giving our assets, there are no strings attached. We can do our thing and move on; we can leave an offering at the altar then continue to live our own life. But God desires it the other way around. He desires for you to first covenant to give to Him your life, your entire being. In doing so, you become empowered to meaningfully share of your time, talent and treasure as He desires.

By freely giving to God, we merely return to Him from what He has already given to us. While we do not give for the sake of getting, God will often use our gifts as the key to unlock the blessings He desires to flow from Him to us. This is especially evident when we make a sacrifice to give when we hardly have enough to supply our own needs.

The widow of Zarephath had this same experience (1 Kings 17:1-16). A famine arose as a result of no rain for a prolonged period of time. This widow had only a small amount of meal and oil remaining and had just gathered 2 sticks to make a cake. This wasn't even enough to spare her life and the life of her son. The widow decided to prepare the meal for the 2 of them to eat, and then wait to die from starvation.

There and then, the prophet Elijah was sent to them by God. God instructed her to feed Elijah from the little she already had. Moreover, she was instructed to feed him first before feeding her own son and herself. The widow obeyed. As a result of her obedience to God, as promised by the prophet Elijah, she miraculously had sufficient oil and meal for her household up until the famine was over.

Instead of failing, the little she had multiplied to supply her needs. She wasn't hesitant to give abundantly to God from the little that she possessed. In return, God did not hesitate to give to her abundantly from the unlimited resources that He possesses. She gave from a faithful heart that desired to honor God's command.

"Prove me now" said the Lord to the Israelites when they were unfaithful in returning their tithes and offering to Him (Malachi 3:7-10). His promise to them in return for their faithfulness is to open the windows of heaven and to pour unto them blessings beyond the scope of what they can receive. God wants you to prove Him. When we are faithful to Him, in one way or another, He will reward our faithfulness.

We may never truly discover the magnitude of our talents, potentials and possessions until we use them towards God's service. We never know the nature and magnitude of what God can accomplish through us until we first make the sacrifice to serve the Lord without reservation.

Even if you do not see where you possess any special ability, try something for the sake of glorifying God and serving others. You may very well discover something new about yourself. Also, the more you exercise your goodwill towards others, the more your skill in service is perfected. Quite often, God will mold our undeveloped talents and increase our meager possessions as we employ them towards His service.

You just have to make that decision to start from somewhere. Sometimes what you have may seem sparing and hardly enough to cover your needs or fulfill a missionary goal. You may therefore question the possibility for you to effectively share with others out of so little. But, like the widow of Zarephath, God magnifies the possession and capabilities of those who live to serve, instead of living for self-gratification.

We were shaped to give. A selfish life that is focused on getting more than in giving is unfulfilling. Such a person will never truly experience the joy that is released with giving. Even in the presence of little, count your blessings. While there will always be those who possess more than you do, there will always be those who possess far less.

You do not have to match the wealth of those who are financially wealthier than you. Aiming for that will only lead you to pattern a selfish lifestyle. Instead, evaluate your own life and how you can share it with others. Evaluate how you can share your life and your assets: time, talent and treasures, with those less fortunate than yourself. While you experience the joy of giving, others will in return, experience joy and love from having their needs attended to by a cheerful giver.

Have you ever wondered why the same item you can easily purchase at a nearby store can bring you far greater delight when gifted to you? This pleasure comes from not just knowing that your needs and wants are being fulfilled. It comes from knowing that you are being thought of and someone cares to take the initiative to put a smile on your face. Share in this delight with someone today. Share this pleasure with the Lord.

Choose to Stand

Time and again, society compels us to fit into existing boxes. This often stifles our individuality and unique traits, but worst of all this can threaten godly principles and even seek to suppress God's ability to use us. After you have found yourself in Christ, you must choose to represent him at all cost. You must choose to stand.

You must choose to be that person God has formed you to be. Choose to represent him with dignity and boldness, even when doing so is not admired by others. You just might never know how God is using your unique life and challenging circumstances to glorify Himself and to bless others.

God does not always fit into existing boxes that society and even religions construct. Serving God wholeheartedly may at times require defying status quo, rocking boats and changing the order of the day. This is just what happened when the 3 Hebrew boys made a decision to remain faithful to God and not to bow in worship to the Babylonian idol, as decreed (Daniel 3).

They could have used a silly excuse to dishonor God. Like probably said: "We prefer not to cause any trouble"; but they didn't. Maybe they could have said: "though we're bowing, we're really worshipping God in our hearts and not the idol"; but they didn't. They could have even said: "it's just a cultural issue, so let's just separate our religion from the act of bowing"; but they didn't.

Instead, they chose to stand! They chose to stand for God at the penalty of their very lives. They would rather stand for God and die, than to dishonor Him and live.

Unlike with these 3 Hebrew boys, many of the conflicts and trials that we encounter today do not pose a threat to our lives. Instead they threaten how well we will be respected and admired within certain circles. Regardless, this still poses a challenge for us to stand for God.

But we must be reminded that when confronted with a moral dilemma and our decision is in favor of securing acceptance and recognition from others instead of in honoring our God, we would be placing them above God in our hearts and lives. We would be automatically trading His presence and influence in our lives for theirs. In choosing to protect our reputation at the expense of honoring God, we would also be placing ourselves above the only true God.

But the 3 Hebrew boys chose to stand for God. When given the death penalty by a fiery grave, God chose to stand with them in the fire. The flames of the fire consumed the men who bound the boys and brought them into the furnace. However, the boys were not consumed. The presence of their life-giving Savior was with them. They never left His presence. Neither did He leave theirs.

Standing is never easy when everyone else seems to be sitting or bowing. It's like paddling against the tide of a rough sea. It's like swimming upstream when it's easier and more conventional to merely flow along with the tide. You will often look stupid to others and might feel stupid even to yourself. You may look as if you are asking for trouble and attracting unnecessary negative attention to yourself. But God will give you the strength to stand once you're willing to stand for Him.

When you choose to be God's ambassador at all cost, He will stand for you at all cost. He will stand with you. He will cover you. He will quench the flames of whatever attack is hurled at you. He will either deliver you from the consequences that follow or empower you to persevere. In any situation that you feel intimidated to represent God as you should, always be reminded: *the Lord is with you - you already have all that you need to stand.*

The True Measurement for Success

After working very hard on what seemed to have been a well-done assignment, a friend of mine was returned a failing grade. How could this have been when she conducted a thorough research and provided a thorough response?

The assessor's feed-back stated that though her response was well-thought out, it wasn't the appropriate response for the question asked. She failed to respond to the question the assessor set before her. From her estimation she met the mark, but based on the assessor's standard - she failed to fulfill his request.

How do you measure success in your own life? Could it be that your measurement for success differs from the Standard of your Life-giver?

As mentioned before, we create our own meanings in life. Therefore, what is success to you may be failure to God. What is failure to you may be success in God's eyes. The same applies with traditions, norms, goals and values set by this world when compared to God's Standard.

For this reason, you may succeed at your own goals but be failing at God's. Therefore, the measure of your success or failure in life in general or in any given situation cannot be based on your own vision or judgment. It cannot be based on the way of this world either. Allow God's Standards to govern your life, as revealed in the Scripture. Let Him be the authoritative source that dictates your:

- Morals
- Life goals
- Decisions
- Success in life

God designed the Plan for your life. He should therefore set the Standard by which the success of this Plan is measured. You cannot set these standards for you. Society cannot set these standards either. Therefore, do not be swayed by the standards of society or others around you. They did not write the script for your life. God knows His plans and requirements for your life. He is therefore, the best director and assessor over your life.

Instead of focusing on other people's expectations of you, why not be guided by God's expectations for your life. Standards set by others might very well conflict with God's. The reality is, you cannot please God and everyone at the same time. When you live to please everyone, you will end up displeasing at least some people and this often includes yourself - and God. Any attempt to please everyone at the same time will interfere with God's authority over your life.

So, you don't have to strive to gain everyone's applaud. At some point in life, you will regret doing so. You will regret not living to be *your* best. You will regret living in accordance with the thwarted prescription the critics laid out for your life.

Like the apostle wrote in Galatians 1:10, a good question to ask yourself is: "Am I now trying to win the approval of human beings, or of God?" Paul continues: "Or am I trying to please people? If I were still trying to please people, I would not be a servant of Christ." You cannot truly follow Christ while living to gain the approval of others.

God is in the best position to dictate the pattern in which your life should take; the battles worth fighting; and the goals worth attaining. Without God's direction, you can spend your lifetime diverting your resources and energy into a particular way of life, path, life goal or projects that prevent you from ever attempting and succeeding in the goals He designed for your life. This happens if you live based on standards outside of God's unique vision for you. It robs you from experiencing the joy and fulfillment that comes with living by God's Standard.

When you feed on the expectations of others, you may succeed in pleasing them. When you feed on the inspiration that this world offers then you just may succeed at what you want. However, when you feed on the Word of God and allow Him to transform you through this knowledge, then you will succeed at what God desires for your life. What are your priorities - the expectations of others, your own will or God's Will for your life?

When God's Will for you becomes your delight, you will find greater contentment in living the life He has blessed you with. In all things, why not seek to be the best that God empowers you to be and trust that in your own right, that's good enough. Be the best that you can possibly be in Christ, without comparison, and be contented that this is enough to qualify you as His achiever (Galatians 6:4). He will empower you according to the measure of achievement He desires for you.

Only you can walk your Journey. You can successfully walk only your Journey - not another person's. We were all shaped differently: to perform uniquely, at different levels and in different capacities. In competing with others for their achievements, you only attempt to trade the unique life that God has blessed you with, for theirs.

But, when through Christ, you seek to be your best; you would have lived your life to the fullest and glorified God astoundingly. Such contentment you will reap out of such a life. Regardless of how seemingly simple these might be, you would have consequently measured up to God's Standard for your life goals and their success.

Always remember that God's Standard for you is based on eternal outcomes.

Bits and Pieces

When you have drunk from the Fountain of Life and have tasted of the very Essence of Life's Journey – everything changes! Life becomes very special, and each passing moment with it. Finding rest in God's joyful presence and fulfilling His Will for your life on this earth now becomes the central focus of your Journey.

Once you are alive, it's never too late for you to find yourself in Christ. It's never too late for you to discover your purpose in Him and reach for it. When you have, it will be the beginning of the best, most rewarding phase of your life.

It would be a shame; however, for you to pass through this earth and never truly experience the joy of being in your Heavenly Father's bosom and the fulfillment from embarking on your life's mission.

One lifetime can seem so short; so short to grow and develop to the stature God envisions for you and to complete the missions He has ordained for your life. However, it all simmers down to how much use you make of the small things in life.

It is a combination of bits and pieces that contribute to the vastness of this world. It is tiny grains of sand that clothe the massive sea shore; it is microscopic cells that form your skin; little droplets of rain that spawn into a great flood; and minute seconds that fill a lifetime... When your minutes, hours, days, weeks and months are intentionally spent wisely and productively with the aim of glorifying God, they accumulate into a lifetime to be reckoned with. Why not get at it this very minute.

Often, it is the tiny steps towards big goals that materialize into great accomplishments; and not necessarily a huge leap. It is in bits and pieces that you will achieve God's overall desires for your life as you journey. Therefore, why not start by focusing on your daily living.

The best start is committing to spending quality time with God each day, and every day. Over time, this will not only build your relationship with Him but also help you to understand how He desires to guide your life and empower you to respond to His guidance.

God may impress something on your heart that might look massive and totally unrealistic. However, tiny objectives towards the fulfillment of long-term goals may prove to be helpful. This may include a day by day or week by week mini-plan. Allow God to direct you in dissecting His goals for you into bits of manageable objectives, as He guides you into His Will for your life.

Setting tiny objectives at the beginning of each day is one way to get long-term goals done without becoming over-loaded and abandoning your goal all together. This can be accomplished either by a mental or written checklist.

A benefit of the written check-list is that you don't have to pressure yourself to remember tasks to be accomplished. Journaling grants you the opportunity to even retrospectively examine how you have been allowing the Lord to master-mind your approach and to influence your Journey. This can also provide a comforting reminder in times when you are confronted with difficulties and easily forget how the Lord has been leading you thus far.

At the end of the day, reflect on the happenings of that day – the accomplishments, the unaccomplished goals, the disappointments and failures. Take the time to express your sincere gratitude for how the Lord has led you so far. Find comfort in Him in dealing with all your failures and disappointments. There is so much that He desires to impart to you through them.

Learn from unaccomplished assignments. Trust the Lord to impress on your mind effective strategies for accomplishing unmet objectives that may require a great deal of energy and dedication. Above all, be reminded that no particular strategy can be compared to ensuring that you are being recreated and that your life is being wholly fuelled and steered by God, moment by moment.

Every day we become one day closer to our final destiny. With your decision, every day you can become one step closer to God in your relationship with

Him and one step closer towards fulfilling your lifelong God-ordained mission.

You are a piece of life's grand puzzle. Your reason for being on this earth is designed into the delicate fabric of life on earth. By choosing to walk with God in accordance with His Will for you, you choose not to change the beautiful, unique pattern that He has meticulously woven for your life. You must take that time to know Him and His Plan for you, deeper and deeper. As you live a life of surrender, Christ will work on you, bit by bit to perfect you as you Journey.

Our individual lives are like the individual pieces of a huge jig saw puzzle. The pieces come in different colors, shapes and sizes yet when positioned in the right place they form a perfect picture. When one is missing from its slot, the picture is never complete. It can never be the same. When you are missing from God's place for you in this life, His grand picture is just not the same. It remains incomplete. Your reason for living would remain unfulfilled. No wonder it is so important for Him to recreate you, redirect and replenish your life and have you occupy your ordained slot on the Narrow Road, right under His Wings.

As you journey in life, make it your main goal to ensure that God is always your all in all. Endeavor to make it your mission to learn from Him your place in this life - His intentions for your life. As life unfolds, allow Him to place you where He desires for you to be. Allow Him to mold you into a vessel of honor for His sacred use and to use you for whatever purpose He chooses.

Then and only then, your life, your little piece in the grand puzzle, would have fitted perfectly into God's picture for humanity. Then and only then, you would have found and experienced the Essence of Life's Journey - and be filled.

Epilogue

"For I know the plans I have for you," declares the LORD, "plans to prosper
you and not to harm you, plans to give you hope and a future."
Jeremiah 29:11

FINDING THE ESSENCE OF your life's Journey is finding God. Basking in the Essence of Life is making God your all in all. It involves journeying intimately with God and having His Will accomplished through your life. This is the sum of the joyful and fulfilling life.

Dare to Dream

Joseph was a dreamer (Genesis 37:5-11). God gave him dreams that he would rule over his siblings and even his parents. His brothers never believed his dreams. They only envied and hated him even more because of these dreams. Joseph; however, never let go of these dreams. For that reason, they all lived to see the fulfillment. These dreams were God's dreams. Once Joseph remained faithful to God, though seemingly impossible, these dreams had to come true.

We may not all be dreamers and interpreters of dreams in the same manner that Joseph was. However, God has dreams or plans for our lives too. He also has unique ways of revealing to us His plans for our unique lives. We must conceptualize these dreams before we can believe them and live them. Do not be afraid to dream big. *The measure of your attainments will never surpass the altitude of the dreams.* Trust God to reveal to you and guide you into His plans for your life, whether great or small.

While growing up, my adolescent brother declared, "Life is so strange. When I was a child all I dreamed of was having a bicycle; now, all I want is to have a car."

Your desires will change as you grow older. Your childhood desires differ from your adolescent desires. Even throughout adulthood and in your Christian Journey as you mature so do your goals and desires. You dare not dream your own dream. Soon, the desire for that dream will die. It's relevance to your life will, at some point, fade. But, the relevance of God's dream for you is eternal.

If you feel that God hasn't yet done so, ask Him to place His dream into your heart. Spend quality time praying and meditating on God's Will for your life and He will guide you into it. Sometimes nobody besides you and God will share that dream. No one else may believe in the reality of that dream being realized. But do not allow this to discourage you.

Hold on to God's dreams. Do not be afraid to trust God to convert these dreams into reality. Like Joseph, God will impress goals and plans on your heart and mind. There is just so much that God wants to achieve in you and through you. Trust Him to use you to achieve His Plans. Joseph had dreams; he believed these dreams, and they came true.

Dare to Believe

The greater the plan that God has for your life, the greater will be the measure of faith that is required to embrace it. God had a great plan for Abraham's life (Genesis 12:1-7; Genesis 15) – A plan that required Abraham to abandon everything that would taint God's ordained purpose. God called Abraham from his country and family, to a strange country. God made a great promise to Abraham that his offspring would possess that foreign country.

Abraham's wife was barren yet God told him to look up at the stars in the sky and assured him that as innumerable as they are, so will be the magnitude of his biological off-springs throughout generations. Abraham didn't own even a plot of land in this foreign country that he was called to, yet God promised Abraham that after 400 years of captivity in another land, his off-spring will return and possess the entire country.

At that time, the fulfillment of this promise seemed absolutely impossible from human reasoning. This is also a promise that would never be fulfilled during Abraham's own life-time. He therefore would have no guarantee of its fulfillment besides his trust in God's words. After the birth of Isaac, his only promised son, Abraham never lived to see him multiply, one generation after another, into a great nation. He never lived to see this nation possess that foreign land, the Promised Land - Canaan.

Abraham had every logical reason to doubt the reality of this promise ever being fulfilled. He could have consequently given up on making himself available for God to use him towards its fulfillment. But he claimed God as his shield and exceeding great reward. He believed in the power and the integrity of God. It was in this that he placed his faith. He made himself available to be used by God as the progenitor of God's master plan. In return, God rewarded this faith.

God's plan for Abraham's life was fulfilled - all because Abraham believed. God's plan for your life will only be fulfilled because you believe. Therefore, always be focused, not on the complexities and impossibilities involved, but on your omnipotent God. Your faith in God will be the factor that converts His plans, His dreams, His goals for your life into a reality. God wants you to dream His dreams. He wants you to go even as far as to believe His dreams. Ultimately, God's desire for you is to live His dreams for your life.

Dare to Live

When we journey with Christ we are no longer spectators of life, standing on the sidelines, watching others live. We become alive and we are empowered to live life to its fullest. We live deeply. Moments of our life will seem longer and are more memorable than many years of empty living combined. Our moments become richer and more meaningful and we're made to recognize that quality or depth of life is far superior to length of life.

Allow Christ to teach you how to live fully, each moment and, every moment of your life. Allow Christ to empower you to live abundantly. Like John the Baptist, you too will be among the greatest of men, born of women. You would have embarked on the Journey planned for you, walked the path paved for you to travel and accomplished the targets set as your life aspirations. You would have abandoned your own plans for your life, in exchange for the life God has designed for you.

Dare to envision God's dream for your life, dare to believe it and dare to live it. The moments of your life will pass, regardless of how you choose to use them. Choose to live them. *Choose to live the joyful and fulfilling life that God designed and ordains for you to live.* Choose to serve your fellow men and to glorify God through your life. Live, live, live abundantly; live life to its fullest.

God envisioned greatness when He conceived you in His mind. Claim this greatness through Jesus Christ. Never lose that intimate connection with God as you journey. As you yield to Him, let God teach you to exploit the Essence of Life's Journey. Regardless of life's challenges, faithfully walk on the Narrow Road with God and His beloved children to the finish line. There will be rejoicing! There will be a grand celebration when you get there.